A Gospel Portrait

Jesus

by Donald Senior, C.P.

Pflaum Publishing,
Dayton, Ohio
1975

ISBN: 0-8278-9003-6
Library of Congress Catalog
Card Number: 75-14636

Designed by Dan Johnson
Printed in the United States of America

Jesus

Contents

Map of Palestine   vii

Introduction   1

1. **Knowing Jesus**   5
   The Gospels as Privileged Sources   9
   The Gospels and Christian Faith   15
   Stage One: Jesus and the Disciples   16
   Stage Two: The Disciples and the Early Church   17
   Stage Three: The Early Church and the Evangelists   20

2. **The World of Jesus**   29
   The Land   30
   The Politics of Jesus' World   33
   Social and Religious Ferment   41

3. **Jesus and His Own**   51
   Jesus and the Kingdom   52
   Jesus and His Disciples   55
   Jesus and the Outcasts   69
   Jesus and Women   74

4. **Jesus Speaks** 83
   The Kingdom Is Coming 83
   The God of the Kingdom 87
   Jesus as Teacher 98
   Jesus and the Law 107

5. **Jesus Heals** 113
   The Meaning of Miracle 115
   Miracles and Ministry of the Kingdom 119
   Miracles and Faith 126

6. **Death and Victory** 133
   The Opposition 136
   Reading the Signs 140
   The Prophet 143
   The Suffering Servant 146
   The Passion Story 152

7. **Jesus and His Church** 159
   The Church Begins 159
   'Beyond' Jesus 161
   Beyond the New Testament 169
   Back to Jesus 170

   Further Reading 177

PALESTINE AT THE TIME OF JESUS

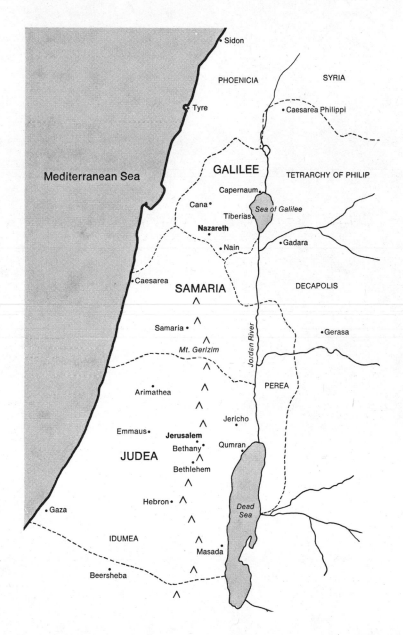

Introduction

Since the turn of the century, our knowledge of the Bible and the world that produced it has taken a quantum leap. Decades of careful analysis have given us new insight into the literary fabric of the Scriptures and the complex process by which Old and New Testaments emerged from Israel and the early church. Countless archaeological explorations and incredible discoveries of ancient letters and documents have provided us with more information about the first century of our era than was available to any generation before us.

But for the Christian who longs to read the New Testament with renewed understanding, much of this information is inaccessible. What may be common knowledge for the professional biblical scholar is locked away in technical journals and heavily footnoted research volumes. The relevance of this material for the average reader of the Bible often is masked by an analysis of seemingly esoteric details and subtle scholarly debate.

The purpose of this book is to bridge some of the most important results of biblical research and the nonprofessional reader. The treatment dwells as much as possible on those aspects of the life and message of Jesus that enjoy a high degree of consensus in the interpretations of contemporary biblical scholars.

Not all of the "technical" questions can or should be

avoided. To a certain degree, the first and last chapters might be considered technical in the sense that they examine some of the suppositions that undergird the intervening chapters. Those middle chapters, which deal directly with the Gospel portrait of Jesus, might be more inviting. But it is important that the reader be acquainted with the sources of that portrait and some of the facts and principles involved in an interpretation of the Gospels.

Still, it is presumed that the reader who turns to this book is not interested in Jesus out of academic curiosity. Many adult Christians today hunger for the Word of God. They sometimes sense that their faith is improperly nourished. For Christians with this sort of hunger, Scripture is food. It nourishes, it satisfies, it gives life. More, it has the power to liberate. The Jesus of the Gospel touches them and frees them from limiting and narrow concepts that dominate their relationship to God and to their brothers and sisters in Christ. So they turn to the Gospels because they want to know more about Jesus and to find in him a source of life and hope.

What do the Gospels say about Jesus? What are some of the things we should know if we want to read the Gospels intelligently? What is some of the history of the first-century world in which Jesus lived and in which the Gospels were written? These are some of the questions that this book attempts to answer by drawing on the results of modern biblical scholarship.

The study begins by analyzing what a Gospel really is. It retraces the long process that took place between the death of Jesus and the appearance of the first written Gospel. The material that the evangelists incorporated into their Gospels first had to pass through the life of the church itself: its preaching, its prayer, its debates, and its teaching. From this basic Gospel tradition, individual evangelists later would fashion coherent "portraits" of Jesus for the audiences to which they addressed their literary masterpieces.

Chapter 1

This book is not a commentary on the Gospels or an attempt to retell the story of Jesus' life. Instead, it sifts through the four Gospels to pinpoint those aspects of the person, the teaching, and the fate of Jesus that were so vital to Christian faith that each of the evangelists had to include them in his portrait of Jesus, no matter how distinctive it might be.

Individual chapters focus on these vital strokes in the Gospel portrait: the touching interaction of Jesus with his chronically dull disciples; the uniqueness of Jesus' association with outcasts and with women; the profound simplicity of his teaching about God, about faith, about forgiveness, about freedom; the significance of the Gospels' testimony that Jesus was a healer and an exorcist; the compelling humanness of Jesus in the face of opposition and death. The study closes by trying to link our own experience as contemporary Christians and members of a church with the challenging freshness of the Gospel portrait.

At a time when there is a growing popular interest in the person of Jesus, and at a time when many Catholics are beginning to turn to the Scriptures to renew their faith, there is a need for help in unlocking the richness of the Gospels. That is what this book tries to do.

Finally, some thanks are in order to those who helped nudge this book to its conclusion. I am grateful to the staff of the Carlow College Summer Institute for the gentle encouragement that kept the wheels turning and to my Passionist brother, Jim Kent, who typed the final manuscript. The results are dedicated to my mother and father whose unselfish love for Miriam has always been gospel for me.

Donald Senior, C.P.
Catholic Theological Union

Knowing Jesus

Is anyone in history more famous than Jesus of Nazareth? Probably not. The power of his reputation over the past 2,000 years has left profound imprints on peoples and cultures. It has built gothic masterpieces, ignited wars, motivated heroic leaders, and even put fluorescent bumper stickers on cars. By far the most significant tribute to the power of Jesus' fame is that countless people claim him as the center of their lives, as the inspiration for their best moments.

In short, a great many people have known and do know about Jesus of Nazareth. Even in places where Christianity is sparse, large numbers of people know about Jesus. The multitude of people who adhere to Islam—a faith that spreads thickly from Northern Africa to Turkey and across the Middle East to Pakistan, India, and Indonesia—know about Jesus from their sacred book, the Koran. This book of Islam has several references to "Jesus, Son of Mary," describing him reverently as one of the greatest of Allah's messengers. Christianity has never had much success in China, but even there people who know something about the Western world know something about the founder of Christianity. So, a case can be made: Great numbers of people know about Jesus of Nazareth.

"Know about . . ." It is not really part of the Christian program that people should simply know *about* Jesus. Genuine Christianity is based on *knowing* Jesus. The urgency of the Christian mission since its beginning has been that people should come to know Jesus personally and, because of that relationship, to transform their lives. To *know* someone in this sense presumes an intimate interlocking of lives and fate. We sense the mystery of another's person. We share with him some of the hidden richness of our own. We are present to each other, and we are able to communicate. Knowledge of this kind is synonymous with friendship and trust. It means a mutual commitment to steadfastness and support. The language of a relationship like this is not curiosity or exploitation but love.

This kind of language comes closest to describing the relationship between the believer and Jesus. The living presence of the Risen Lord in the world of today is unique, mysterious, even baffling. But the instinct of the Christian believer tells him or her that the living presence of Jesus is something more than the echo of his fame. It is even something more than the force of his example. The life of Jesus Christ tells us much about what it means to be a human being. But the unique assertion of faith is that the presence of Jesus gives the believer the transforming power to *be* more human.

The reality of the living presence of Jesus is, in some ways, ineffable. But the experience of faith undergirds a conviction that it is real—a surge of peace in a moment of prayer, the transforming power of genuine forgiveness, the infectious strength of another believer. These are the moments, however rare, when we touch the reality of the presence of Jesus.

The believer, then, already knows Jesus, however fragile that knowledge might seem. We already have placed in him, almost unconsciously, our ultimate hopes for life and peace. For those of us who *know* Jesus in all the varying degrees of the spectrum, to learn *about* Jesus can be a confirmatory experience. All of us realize from experience that knowing a person, in the sense we have been describing, can precede "knowing about" him. We can be drawn into genuine friendship with someone before we really know much about him or her—perhaps through a shared moment of crisis or of genuine delight, perhaps by silent observation over a long period of time. A set of gestures, a way of looking or being can capture love, and two people begin the long road to genuine friendship. In this situation, "knowing about" is a secondary stage. Love causes a great hunger to know about the object of love. We want to know about his or her past, friends, opinions, habits. And where the instinct of love has been right, each new act of "knowing about" can be a delicious discovery. A gradual pulling back of a curtain reveals that the image of the person we had drawn in our heart was right. To learn things about the person we love often can be, then, not a mere assembling of a biographical file but a discovery that fortifies and confirms a deep knowing already present.

This process of discovery and confirmation describes much of our experience of friendship, of love. It also describes the experience that many Christians have as their faith matures. Years of faith build up a relationship to Jesus that we should not underestimate, especially for ourselves. Even if our faith is tenuous and neglected, we still accumulate expectations of Jesus. Thus, over a long period of time, a personal "portrait" of Jesus takes shape. It is formed by the example of families and friends, by the teaching we have been exposed to, even by the architecture and music that are part of our Christian heritage. But our own longings and reflection add strokes to the portrait as well, even if we have not reflected on the process.

Let me give an example. Almost everyone has felt the smothering sense of shame that accompanies being "caught in the act." Something we said or did was patently wrong, and suddenly all the world knows. There is no escape. We feel helpless, ashamed. If it was something seriously wrong, the sense of guilt may be paralyzing and destructive. Human response to someone "caught in the act" can be cruel. The ridicule of laughter or the cut of a righteous stare compounds the burden of shame. The person caught is an easy target.

How would Jesus deal with someone "caught in the act"? The question is not very challenging. Instinctively we would expect of him a sensitive compassion, with no trace of righteousness or cruelty. We would expect only a protective mercy that would reach out to shield the vulnerability of the one caught. Our portrait of Jesus tells us he would be like that. And "knowing about" him confirms our instinct. The pages of the Gospels reveal a Jesus whose sensitivity to guilt and shame never falters. The incident of Jesus and the woman caught in adultery comes to mind. In chapter eight of John's Gospel, we are presented with the classic situation. Righteous moralists do not hesitate to exploit the woman's shame to make their point. "Teacher, this woman has been caught in the act of adultery. In the law, Moses ordered such women to be stoned. What do you have to say about the case?" For Jesus, the woman is not a "case"; she is a person. He refuses to join their mockery. Their righteousness crumbles against his eloquent silence. Their contrived indignation defused, they leave the scene. The woman is left with the compassion of Jesus. It is not a cheap compassion; his reaction is clear: You are not condemned; but also, sin no more. To read and reflect on this touching Gospel incident confirms our expectations of Jesus.

To learn about Jesus may not always be so comforting. The image of Jesus with which we begin may not be totally accurate. Sometimes too much of ourselves is reflected in the portrait. Thus our Jesus may be too familiar, too middle class, too white, or too revolutionary. Often it is a case of our image of Jesus being immature. The portrait we have of him—and as a result, our relationship with him—has not kept pace with our own growth. Even as adults we can still think of Jesus in ways that we did as children. The image may be comforting, but it may not sustain us and challenge us as adults. Thus the experience of learning about Jesus is not only confirmatory, but it can have the effect of discovery, even judgment.

The necessity of deepening and sharpening our faith portrait of Jesus points to the Gospels. Here every Christian's image of Jesus must find its validation. Not everything that must be said about Jesus and about genuine Christian life is found in the Gospels. But the *source* of everything we know about Jesus and the test of genuineness for every aspect of Christian life and teaching ultimately are found in the Gospels. The New Testament—and, as we shall see, the Gospels in particular—is the lifeline that links Jesus of Nazareth with people of every age who claim to be his disciples.

Many adult Christians are discovering this fact on their own. Anyone who has taken part in adult education or Bible study groups knows what I mean. Many adult Christians who sense that their faith needs to mature and to grow experience a great sense of liberation and discovery when they read and reflect on the Scriptures. The portrait of Jesus found in the Gospels not only confirms the best instincts of their faith, but it gives that image new life and vividness. To know Jesus in a truly Christian way—as free as possible of our own subjectivity—we ultimately must know him from the Gospels, the source of that portrait.

The Gospels as Privileged Sources

Before attempting to draw out the Gospel portrait of Jesus, it might be worth considering the nature of these literary works on which so much of our faith depends. Why are they so crucial? What is their power? These fundamental questions about the Gospels should be faced; much of what we are able to say about Jesus depends on understanding what a Gospel is.

The most obvious reason for turning to the Gospels to discover an authentic portrait of Jesus is that they are practically all we have! The simple fact is that unless we had the Gospels, our knowledge of Jesus of Nazareth would be a dim rumor in the corridors of history.

Non-biblical witness to Jesus is very scarce, although the record is not entirely blank. Several references to Jesus, or at least to the impact of his life, are found in the writings of Roman authors. Such is the case with Suetonius, a writer who compiled the biographies of several Roman emperors around the year 120 A.D. In his account of the life of the Emperor Claudius, he refers to the expulsion of the Jews from Rome in A.D. 49: "He expelled the Jews from Rome, on account of the riots in which they were constantly indulging, at the instigation of Chrestus." It is generally believed that the name "Chrestus" is a mistaken reference to *Christus* or Christ. At this early date, the Christians were still viewed by most Roman authorities as a sect of Judaism. We know very little about the circumstances Suetonius describes, although the comment of Luke in the Acts of the Apostles (18:2) that Aquila, a Jew, had come to Corinth "because Claudius had commanded all the Jews to leave Rome" bears out his testimony. Suetonious' report about Jesus is inaccurate, of course; Jesus was never at Rome. But the reference does stand as an independent reference to Jesus at a very early date.

Another Roman historian, Tacitus, also refers to Jesus. His Roman annals, written about 115 A.D., mention Nero's attempt to blame the Christians for the burning of Rome in 64 A.D. Tacitus was skeptical of Nero's story, but he had little use for the Christians who suffered from it. His distaste for Christians has left us this fascinating reference to Jesus:

They got their name from Christ, who was executed by sentence of the procurator Pontius Pilate in the reign of Tiberius. That checked the pernicious superstition for a short time, but it broke out afresh—not only in Judaea, where the plague first arose, but in Rome itself, where all the horrible and shameful things in the world collect and find a home.

It is interesting that almost all of the early Roman documents referring to Christ and Christians are records of disturbances or police action. The Roman state was notoriously suspicious of political associations, and the close-knit Christian communities, with their mysterious beliefs and practices, could only have baffled the nervous Roman authorities. Such, in fact, is the testimony of the letter of Pliny the Younger, written around A.D. 111. Pliny, whose voluminous correspondence has earned him literary fame, was appointed legate to the Roman province of Bithynia, in the northwest section of what is present-day Turkey. He frequently consulted the Emperor Trajan on policy matters. One letter that has been preserved concerns the proper method for dealing with Christians. Twice in the letter Pliny refers to Christ, although no direct information is given about his life or teaching.

Pliny indicates that his method for dealing with those accused of being Christians was to demand that they recant by "cursing Christ" and offering homage to the emperor. He adds that through torture he had extracted from two female deacons the information that, among other things, the members of this sect sang hymns to "Christ as God."

Early Jewish documents outside of the New Testament that refer to Jesus are equally sparse. The problem with evaluating these documents as independent witnesses to Jesus' life is their date. Most of the sayings of the early rabbis and their intricate commentaries on the Jewish Law were codified in written form only in later centuries. Thus even early traditions that might reach back to the time of Jesus or the early church have been influenced by the intervening tension between Jews and Christians. As we will see, the same sort of difficulty must be faced in regard to the Gospels themselves.

One of the Jewish texts most frequently quoted about Jesus is taken from the Babylonian Talmud; it represents a tradition that may go as far back as the first or second century:

Jesus was hanged on Passover Eve. Forty days previously the herald had cried, "He is being led out for stoning, because he has practiced sorcery and led Israel astray and enticed them into apostasy. Whosoever has anything to say in his defense, let him come and declare it." As nothing was brought forward in his defense, he was hanged on Passover Eve.

The context for this passage is a discussion of Jewish law, hence there is no reference to the Roman role in the execution of Jesus. To be "hanged" ordinarily refers to hanging as we know it; but it does not exclude crucifixion, i.e., "hanging on the cross." The emphasis on Jesus' guilt and on the fact that adequate grounds for a defense had been allowed indicates a sensitivity to some of the Christian accusations regarding the manner in which Jesus died. But this text and a few similar ones from later rabbinic writings really do not give us much information about Jesus or his teaching. And it is doubtful whether the information they provide flows directly from Jewish witness contemporary with Jesus or whether it is a later Jewish response to Christian preaching and apologetic.

Josephus, the renowned historian of the first century, is difficult to fit into either Jewish or Roman camp. Born and raised a Palestinian Jew, Josephus deserted his countrymen during the Jewish revolt of 67-73 A.D. and joined the invading Roman forces. Later, after carefully currying the favor of a succession of Roman emperors, Josephus wrote an extensive account of Jewish history and of the Roman suppression of the first-century Jewish revolt. Strangely enough for a renegade, Josephus' purpose was to try to present Jewish thought and actions in the best light possible to his Roman sponsors. He also had one eye on his

Jewish compatriots; he hoped to justify to them his allegiance to the Roman emperor. Thus the accuracy of Josephus' historical writings often has been viewed with skepticism, particularly by Jewish readers. Despite his pronounced bias, however, Josephus does provide us with a mass of valuable information about the first century.

Twice in his collection called *Antiquities*, Josephus refers to Jesus. In a passage dealing with the death of James, the early leader of the Christian church in Jerusalem, Josephus mentions that James was a brother "of Jesus the so-called Christ" (*Antiquities*, book 20, 200). A much more detailed reference to Jesus appears in book 18 of the *Antiquities*:

Now, there was about this time Jesus, a wise man, if it be lawful to call him a man, for he was a doer of wonderful works, a teacher of such men as receive the truth with pleasure. He drew over to him both many of the Jews, and many of the Gentiles. He was the Christ. And when Pilate, at the suggestion of the principal men amongst us, had condemned him to the cross, those that loved him at the first did not forsake him; for he appeared to them alive again at the third day; as the divine prophets had foretold these and ten thousand other wonderful things concerning him. And the tribe of Christians, so named from him, are not extinct at this day.

The difficulty with relying on this remarkable tribute to Jesus is that most scholars agree that it has been touched up by later *Christian* writers. It is simply unthinkable that a Jew-turned-Roman of the first century would refer to Jesus as someone more than a man or baldly identify him as "the Christ." The passage reads like a Christian testimony to Jesus, and that most probably is what it is. More than likely, the original text of Josephus was far less complimentary (note the sarcasm of "Jesus the so-called Christ" in book 20), and later Christian writers spruced up the text to make it inoffensive to believers.

Thus one comes back from a search through early, non-biblical archives practically empty-handed. But this could be expected; we have little information about *any* individuals who lived in the first century A.D. And it is perfectly normal that Christians themselves would be the ones to transmit most of the information about Jesus. Only gradually did the Roman empire and other segments of the non-Christian world begin to feel the impact of Jesus of Nazareth as the number of his followers began to mushroom with incredible rapidity.

No one could build much of a portrait of Jesus from the incidental references in Roman and Jewish documents. So we must return to the New Testament and ultimately to the Gospels. The New Testament, as we know, is not a uniform book or collection of volumes. It offers a variety of materials: personal letters, religious tracts, liturgical homilies, and the Gospels themselves. Among all of this literature, only the Gospels present the life history of Jesus in any detailed way. If we screen the letters of Paul, for example, we can find some basic facts about the life of Jesus: that he lived and died in Palestine, that he gathered disciples, that he was crucified by the Romans with the Jewish leaders as instigators. But Paul never gives us any narration about incidents in the life of Jesus—with the possible exception of the account of the Eucharist, a tradition Paul quotes in 1 Corinthians, chapter 11. Only occasionally does he allude to specific sayings of Jesus.

Paul's concern is the significance of Jesus' death and resurrection for Christian life. He spells out this concern not by reviewing the details of Jesus' history but by reflecting on the dynamics of redemption. The other New Testament authors in this respect are similar to Paul. None of them is a "storyteller" in the way the Gospel writers are. To a certain extent, they attempt to paint a portrait of the Christian rather than a portrait of Jesus.

The Gospels and Christian Faith

The power of the Gospels to shape our faith portrait of Jesus does not depend solely on the fact that they are a unique source of information about the life of Jesus. In fact, an overemphasis on the Gospels as sources of biographical information about Jesus could distort our understanding of what they are and thus blunt their power. As is often repeated today by New Testament scholars, the Gospels are not "biographies" in the technical sense. We do not do full justice to the nature and purpose of a Gospel, nor do we really learn how to read it, if we expect of it the same sort of detached description of historical events that we might expect of a modern biography.

If a Gospel is not technically a biography, then what is it? Since throughout this book we will be drawing on the Gospels for our portrait of Jesus, it is important that we face this question now. Perhaps the best way to understand the nature of a Gospel is to understand the process by which it was composed. Many Christians may never have reflected on the origin of the Gospels. And, sometimes, the ideas that we do have can block a sound appreciation of the nature of a Gospel.

On the wall of my office hangs a painting that I treasure; it was a gift from my parents when I received my doctoral degree. The painting is a copy of a medieval portrait of the evangelist Matthew. The scene is familiar. Matthew, a venerable old man with flowing beard and bald head, bends over a writing desk where a large parchment scroll is spread before him. The evangelist is not alone. A classic angel with wings and flowing white garment stands beside Matthew, one arm around the evangelist's shoulder and the other firmly guiding his hand as words flow from a quill pen. A heavenly glow illumines the face of Matthew and his angelic muse. Few of us would have trouble interpreting the message of this painting. Matthew is writing his Gospel. The angel symoblizes the divine guidance or "inspiration" that certifies that the Gospel

Matthew is writing is not an ordinary book but our sacred Scripture, the word of God. The painting's testimony to the Gospels as our sacred book is something no believer would contest. The problem with the painting's image is not the values it seeks to communicate but the *process* of composing a Gospel that it implies.

Too often the working image we have of a Gospel is close to that of the anonymous Flemish artist who painted my picture: The evangelist was a mere secretary for divine dictation, and a Gospel is a book that practically dropped from heaven. In fact, the process by which the Gospels came into existence was much more complex—and much richer—than the rather magical procedure implied in this picture. And the more we know about the real process, the more we can understand how to read a Gospel and how to savor the portrait of Jesus it provides.

Perhaps the soundest way to grasp what a Gospel is and how it came to be written is to retrace what has come to be known as the three stages in the transmission of the Gospel material. This analysis of the Gospel process is the fruit of much detailed New Testament scholarship over the past half century. It represents the broadest areas of consensus among students of the Gospels, and its general outline has been accepted in Catholic circles. Ten years ago, in an important document entitled *The Historical Truth of the Gospels,* the Vatican commission that oversees Catholic research on the Bible endorsed these three stages as a sound method of analysis. This endorsement is echoed in Vatican Council II's document on Revelation.

Stage One: Jesus and the Disciples

The Gospels find their roots in the life and mission of Jesus of Nazareth. This statement might seem obvious to most readers, but it should not be forgotten. If the Gospels are to be of any real value to the believer who considers Jesus as the revelation of God, then the Gospel portrait of Jesus must reflect in a credible way the words and works of Jesus himself. If not, if the interpretation of later history brings us to a Jesus who does not reflect the man who walked the roads of Palestine, then the Incarnation becomes a strange assertion of Christian faith.

Thus the Gospel material, the basic content from which the Gospels were composed, finds its root in the life history of Jesus. But not Jesus alone. Jesus chose disciples. He interacted with his opponents. Much of the Gospel record includes reaction to Jesus as well as his own message and actions. And if the life and message of Jesus were to survive his death, then it would be up to his disciples, those entrusted with his memory and message, to proclaim Jesus to others. It was the disciples who transmitted the Gospel material to the second stage.

Stage Two: The Disciples and the Early Church

To understand this stage in the formation of the Gospels, we have to realize that writing the Gospels and the rest of the New Testament was not the first item on the early community's agenda. In fact, it was several decades before any of the New Testament writings appeared. The first thing the early disciples of Jesus did after the death and resurrection of Jesus was not to write but to live and proclaim the message entrusted to them. The conviction that Jesus was alive, that he was the Christ, the fullness of God's promise, ignited a missionary campaign whose energy and success perhaps have never been equaled. The rapidly expanding Christian community was convinced that Jesus' victory over death had ushered in a new age, an age that signaled that the completion of God's creation was fast approaching. The rationale of the Christian mission was to proclaim Jesus' victory and to urge everyone to reform his life in the face of this new and critical age.

The energy and conviction of this Christian mission carried the faith across the frontiers of Palestine where it had originated into the Roman empire—Egypt, Greece, Asia Minor, Syria, Mesopotamia—and into the capital city itself. With awesome force, Christian life flowed out into the Mediterranean world and beyond.

Given the rapid and enthusiastic expansion of the early Christian church—and the fact that it expected a quick end to the world—it is not surprising that these Christians neglected to produce written records. There was little point in writing histories or preserving archives for a future that had little chance of being realized. The focus was the present.

But if the future was in some way neglected, the past was not. The past gave meaning to the present. The past was the record of God's saving acts and his promises in the Old Testament. The past was the fulfillment of those promises in the life, death, and resurrection of Jesus. This basic conviction—that the life of Jesus fulfilled the promise of God—became the fundamental message of much of the early Christian preaching, as we can note from the basic outline of the missionary sermons in the book of Acts (cf. 2:14-36, 3:12-26, etc.).

Here, in the preaching and life of this dynamic missionary church, we discover how the memory of Jesus' life history was kept alive. Incidents from the life of Jesus were used in preaching and catechizing to initiate or strengthen faith. Reflection on the words and actions of Jesus in the light of the Old Testament became an important part of Christian worship. The incisive wisdom of Jesus' words helped Christians deal with the baffling problems and decisions that engulfed the new community as it crossed frontiers of culture and religious background.

Thus the material that later would be used in the composition of the Gospels was not lost or forgotten during this stage of the community's life. This material guided and uplifted the faith of the early Christians. But this material was not in the exact form that it would take when it was put together in a Gospel. Stories about Jesus existed in isolated units, as examples in preaching, much as they are in our liturgy today. Words of Jesus were applied to specific situations or moral questions, but they were not always connected with some specific historical setting in the life of Jesus. So the Gospel material was not maintained within the framework of a coherent life history of Jesus. Much of it was free-floating and isolated. The general outline of Jesus' life of preaching in Galilee and of his death in Judea was well known, but no written biography of Jesus had been produced. Nor did the early Christians seem to think it necessary to have one.

The words and works of Jesus treasured in the life of the early church and eventually handed on to future generations did not remain untouched by their use in the community. The tradition was a living tradition that not only uplifted the life of the believers; it in turn was shaped and effected by its use in the church.

One of the most important of these "changes" is the very selection of material. Not all of the available information about Jesus was preserved. We know very little in fact about the kind of things that would satisfy our curiosity. We do not know, for example, the color of Jesus' hair or his facial appearance. We know almost nothing about his youth and very little about his family. Much of this material was soon lost from memory because, as we stated, the early Christians were not intent on building up a biographical file on Jesus. The memories they treasured and utilized in their preaching and church life were only those words and works of Jesus that had the power to transform lives.

The material that was preserved was shaped according to the use the early church made of it. Unnecessary details were filtered out of miracle stories, for example. What remains in almost all of the Gospel accounts is a barebones narration of the essentials: the plight of the sick person, the response of Jesus, the reactions of disciples, bystanders, or opponents. The words of Jesus are lean and to the point; they bear the sure traces of countless repetition. Many of the stories that recount Jesus' conflicts with his opponents over points of law are barely stories at all but narrative frameworks on which to hang the pointed replies of Jesus. Very often the Christian practice of reflecting on Jesus' life against the backdrop of Old Testament prophecy has bonded New Testament incident and Old Testament allusion so closely together that now they can hardly be pried apart. Such is the case in the Passion story with its countless Old Testament images and allusions.

We will return to many of these examples in the course of drawing out the Gospel portrait of Jesus. We refer to them now simply to illustrate that the very material we have in the Gospels has been touched by the faith and experience of the early Christians who transmitted their precious heritage to us.

Stage Three: The Early Church and the Evangelists

With the third stage we come to that point in the formation of the Gospels that the Flemish artist mentioned above attempted to depict. But our movement through the first two stages already suggests that important modifications must be made in the artist's conception of the process.

First, it is unlikely that any of the Gospels represent the penned memories of an eyewitness, even under the guidance of inspiration. The first Gospel to be written, that of Mark, did not come into existence until around the mid-sixties, some 30 years after the death of Jesus. The tradition that assigns the apostolic names of Matthew and John to two of the Gospels is a later tradition that does not seem supported by the tenor of those Gospels themselves —certainly not in the sense that these Apostles literally put the written Gospels into their final form. Thus the Gospels do not represent an attempt simply to preserve as accurately as possible eyewitness memories of Jesus. They are something much more.

Second, as our outline of the process suggests, the

evangelist depended on the fund of material preserved by and circulating in the life of his church. Mark and the other evangelists after him formed their Gospels from material that already had been touched by the life of the church. The contribution of the evangelist was first to draw together this material that had existed, for the most part, in isolated units into a coherent life story of Jesus. In a sense, the work of the evangelists ran counter to the natural tendency of the second-stage use of the material. The use of the many words of Jesus and incidents from his life in preaching, in liturgy, and in catechetics would tend to fragment the tradition, to give the material a host of different shadings and forms as the Christian mission moved into new situations and languages. The evangelists, by gathering the material together and by fitting it into an overall narrative framework of the life of Jesus, countered this splinter effect and helped preserved the Gospel content from excessive fragmentation.

But the evangelists were not mere collectors of vignettes about Jesus, assembling words of Jesus and stories from his life like beads on a string. A Gospel is not some sort of family album in which memories of the past are lovingly glued onto a page. Some of the motivation for writing the Gospels admittedly may have been to put in more permanent form traditions about Jesus that might be lost for future generations if allowed to float freely in the oral tradition of the church. By the latter half of the first century, when the Gospels started to appear, the church had begun to realize that it would be around for an indefinite period of time. In the later writings of the New Testament, including the pastoral letters to Timothy and Titus as well as the Gospels, there is evidence that the church had started to organize itself in a more permanent fashion and was concerned about handing on its heritage to future generations. But still, the prime purpose of the Gospels was not to record history. Just as the early preachers had used the words and deeds of Jesus to uplift and instruct their audiences, so too the evangelists used their Gospels as messages for their churches.

The Gospel as written by Mark or Matthew or Luke or John was not composed for the wide world or to be included in some universal collection of church literature. The Gospel writers had a much more immediate purpose. They gathered together the traditions about Jesus available to them in their particular locale and put them together into a coherent story, a literary whole, in such a way that it would speak eloquently to the problems and hopes of the community of Christians they served. Mark seems to have been the first Christian to attempt this unique type of message. Matthew and Luke borrowed many things from Mark, but each added important additions and alterations of his own. John probably wrote somewhat later, and he seems to have a fund of tradition independent of the other three. But in each case, the evangelist put together a portrait of Jesus that would speak to the faith of his church.

The role of the evangelist, then, is something like that of the classical prophets of the Old Testament. Prophets like Isaiah or Jeremiah were not prophets in the sense of soothsayers, predicting the future with eerie accuracy. Rather, they were men who had a strong sense of the *past*, who understood thoroughly the religious heritage of Israel and were not afraid to apply that heritage with all of its implications to the present situation of their community. The evangelists did the same. As men of faith, they drew on the tradition of the church and shaped it in such a way that it spoke boldly and eloquently to the present. The tradition they used was not theological speculation about the meaning of Christian life or musings about the nature of God or Jesus but traditions about Jesus' life, his words, his actions, the reactions of disciples, opponents, and crowds. These were put together in such a way that each Gospel portrait of Jesus had a deep impact on the community for whom it was written.

Thus each of the Gospels is unique—not only because it was composed by a different writer but because the situations to which it was addressed were different. Was the community in which Mark found himself suffering persecution and apostasy? Then Mark's portrait of Jesus was heavily toned with an emphasis on the passion and its meaning for discipleship. Did the Jewish Christians of Matthew's church wonder about their obligation to the Jewish Law? Did they struggle with the baffling tragedy of Israel's rejection of the Gospel while gentiles were flooding into the church, all of this apparently the opposite of what God's promises in the Old Testament had led them to expect? Then Matthew's portrait brought the healing power of Jesus the teacher whose wisdom fitted all into the saving plan of God. And so on with the rest of the Gospels.

Once we understand what the evangelist was trying to do, we can no longer be content with labeling the Gospels as "histories." The Gospels are not history books but "gospel." This term, meaning "good news," was first applied to the preaching of the early church as it proclaimed Jesus' victory over death. The genius of the evangelists was to apply that term to the *life story* of Jesus. And they did it with full justification; the portrait of Jesus that they presented to their churches was meant to be a penetrating message of life just as much as the sermons of the first missionaries.

A survey of these three stages in the production of the Gospels identifies the missing element in the Flemish picture of the evangelist Matthew. The missing element is the church. The four Gospels were not presented to the early church as heavenly blueprints for the course of action it should take as it stepped out into the world. It was the other way around. First came the *church*, the community of believers charged with faith in Jesus and his words of life. The Gospels, in a real sense, were the product of the church's life: The church maintained the memory of Jesus and his mission. The church and its experience selected and preserved those moments of Jesus' life that meant the most to a believer. The church etched its own rich experience onto the very contents of the Gospel. And, finally, from the church came the evangelists, those creative men to whom we are indebted for the Gospels. Thus the Gospels, and the entire New Testament, are truly a "book of the church."

Years of patient scholarship have helped us understand a lot more about the complex process through which a Gospel came to be written. We know that when an evangelist picked up his quill pen, he was not depending simply on his memory but on the faith experience of generations of Christians.

But if we can explain the evangelist and his pen, can we explain the "angel"? Our medieval portraitist tried to account for the guidance of the Spirit—and thus the reliability of what Matthew wrote—by giving a prominent place at the writing desk to an angel, symbolic of God's inspiration. Almost all theologians and Scripture scholars today admit that a renewed understanding of how the Gospels were composed calls for a renewed understanding of what we mean by "inspiration." In the past, we may have concentrated too much on the individual writer and his piece of parchment, placing divine inspiration somewhere in between. At some point in the process, an individual did have to write out the final form of a Gospel. But crucial steps already had taken place before this moment, steps that had shaped and sealed much of the message the evangelist would transmit. Inspiration—by which we simply mean the guidance of the Spirit—must be as extensive and diffuse as the process we have traced. The focus of inspiration must be not only the individual but the church itself. The power of the Spirit was present in the church's preaching, in its worship, in its teaching. The power of the Spirit guided the young Christian church as it pushed out into an unknown future. The power of the

Spirit, above all, helped maintain in the church a living memory of Jesus' words and works. The power of the Spirit of God gave the church the authority to keep in mind Jesus' words and actions not as a touching memory from the past but as a living presence, a presence that allowed the community to find new relevance in the ministry of Jesus as the church faced new situations.

In short, perhaps the most crucial consideration we can make about the Gospels and the early church is that the portrait of Jesus handed on to us is truly credible— credible in the sense that it faithfully conveys to us who Jesus was and what he was about, credible in the sense that this portrait reveals the Risen Lord who is with his church for all times and in all places.

As we turn now to search out some of the lines of this Gospel portrait, we might keep in mind some reflections this first chapter prompts.

First, the evidence tells us that if we want to know more about Jesus, we must turn to the Gospels. They are the privileged source for the life of Jesus. Anything the church or the individual Christian asserts about Jesus must be authenticated in the light of the Gospels. If a Christian longs to deepen his or her love for Jesus Christ by knowing more about him, then he or she must turn finally to the Gospels. There is no other portrait worthy of our faith.

But, at the same time, an understanding of what a Gospel is and how it came to be written tells us that we should not seek in the Gospels something we cannot find. We will not find a Jesus free of his church. A modern journalist like Jim Bishop might be able to write a book entitled *The Day President Kennedy Was Shot* that provides us with a minute-by-minute recital of a crucial day in history. He can do so because his sources and his purpose make it possible. The Gospels are not like that. The picture of Jesus they present is not a videotape but a portrait. And we have not one portrait but four. Thus the best way to learn about Jesus is not to spend too much time attempting to retell from beginning to end the life story of Jesus. This method, attempted so often in the past, can lead to frustration and can even distort our understanding of Jesus. A much richer way, one that fits the nature of the Gospels, is to see what the common features are that cut across all four New Testament portraits of Jesus. What is there about the person and ministry of Jesus that each of the evangelists, no matter what the particular situation of his church, felt compelled to include in his Gospel message? The chapters that follow attempt to find these common brush strokes on the New Testament canvas.

Another question prompted this opening chapter: Why are the Gospels so powerful? Why do they have the force of discovery and confirmation for the believer who seeks to enrich his or her faith in Christ? The answer is a tautology: The Gospels are powerful because they are powerful! An understanding of what a Gospel is helps explain this. The Gospels have the power to enrich our faith because that precisely is their purpose. As noted, the Gospels draw the bulk of their content from the very life of the church. It was not incidental items of curiosity that the living memory of the church preserved about Jesus but those words and actions powerful enough to reach into the heart of the believer and to give life. When a Christian picks up a Gospel and reads it with a searching faith, he is duplicating the very process by which it came to be written. As someone has noted, the Gospels are written "from faith to faith." "From faith" in the sense that it was the faith of the church that maintained the genuine portrait of who Jesus was and what he was about. "To faith" in the sense that the Gospels were written so that the belief of Christians might intensify as they came face to face with the words and actions of the Risen Lord.

Thus to read a Gospel as it was meant to be read involves the very elements that produced it: a church that gives meaning and context for what we read, faith that finds there nourishment and life, the Spirit who breathes meaning into our Christian existence. The ultimate purpose of everything written in this book is to encourage the reader to be caught up in that cycle and thereby to discover the compelling beauty of Jesus Christ.

Chapter 2

The World of Jesus

Anyone who begins to search out the Gospel portrait of Jesus will soon discover the baffling traces of another world. Jesus was not a 20th-century man but a Jew of the first century. The Gospel story is full of strange people and parties, unfamiliar lands and places, conflict and debate whose point and emotion have been tempered with centuries of receding time. The more we want to know about Jesus, the more we should know about his world.

Jesus, as the Gospels tell it, seems to conduct his ministry in a mobile arena constantly ringing with debate: Pharisees, Sadducees, Herodeans, high priests, elders. There is talk of ritual washing of hands and of numerous subtleties of Sabbath law. Around the circle of the arena swirl the crowds—some curious, some grateful, some pleading: publicans, sinners, tax collectors, prostitutes, fishermen, scribes, lawyers, the sick. Ominous rumblings break through the din in the arena to suggest a backdrop of imminent political crisis: a Roman prefect sits in judgment in the Jewish capital city; a Jewish vassal king rules the northern region of Galilee. We hear of rebels and riots, of executions and punishment. We sense the tension of a land occupied by a foreign power. Well-worn prejudices flash frequently into speech and gesture: Galileans are mocked for their accent; Nazareth is called a city with no expectations; Samaritans are feared, hated, and avoided.

And then there is the geography on which all of this is played, a string of names and places vaguely familiar but mostly without identity or character for us. But for Jesus and his compatriots, they were real: Capernaum, Nazareth, Jericho, Bethany, Jerusalem, Emmaus, Tiberias, Caesarea, the Ten Cities, Tyre, and Sidon. And we catch something of the land's face: the mountains where Jesus seeks solitude from the din of his mission, the desert, the river Jordan, the rich farmland, the ever-present Lake of Galilee. Seldom do the Gospels step back from their narration to reflect explicitly on all of this. Some of the evangelists may have been as unfamiliar with this scene as we are. The names and places and factions are part of the story, the Gospel tradition about Jesus, and they flow on without explanation.

But the very inclusion of these bits and pieces of background reveals an important feature of the Gospel portrait of Jesus. Jesus was not a mythical God whose fabled life was played out in a timeless kingdom. He was a man whose birth and life and death were bounded by the observable limits of time and place. Much of what Jesus thought and said and did was in reaction to the culture and situation of his countrymen. If we hope to read his portrait with intelligence and understanding, then we must know something about the thoroughly human dimensions of Jesus' world. This, after all, is part of taking seriously our belief in the Incarnation.

The Land

The land shapes people and their history. The small tract of land that held the life of Jesus had much to do with the fate of his countrymen and his own place in it.

Israel, or Palestine (the name given to the region by the ancient Greeks in reference to the Philistines who inhabited the coastal area), was a small tract on the world map at the time of Jesus, a narrow rectangular strip, scarcely 150 miles long and only 50 to 60 miles wide at its broadest point (see map page vii). The land's strategic importance belied its size. It formed the keystone of the so-called "fertile crescent," the land bordering the southeastern rim of the Mediterranean Sea that served as the corridor alternately for Syria and Persia's moves west and Egypt's moves east. Later, it became the threshold for the eastward expansion of Greece and then of Rome. Israel was a land tatooed with the invader's boot.

The Bible speaks of Israel as the "land of milk and honey." Those products existed there certainly, but the phrase's connotation must have been taken with wry humor by the inhabitants of that rough and craggy land. The land's backbone is humped with mountains, rising to 9,000 feet in the north and still precipitous in the south. On each side of this central ridge, the surface tapers into flat land, an arable coastal strip on the west and rugged barren desert to the east. A single precious river, the Jordan, parallels the central ridge, separating the mountains from the desert. The Jordan begins in the high mountains of the north, widens suddenly into the Sea of Galilee, narrows again, and lays a hesitant strip of green along the border of the desert until it spills into the brackish salt waste of the Dead Sea, the lowest point on earth. Where the river dies, the desert stretches without interruption to the Arabian gulf, over a hundred miles to the south.

The cool green of the Sea of Galilee and the salt wastes of the Dead Sea reveal the differing personalities of the extremities of Israel. Galilee, the northern region surrounding the lake, is a lush land of rolling hills. A narrow plain on the western side of the lake, Gennesareth, has been famous from ancient times until now for its fertility. The well-stocked lake nourished a thriving fishing industry even in Jesus' day when pickled and dried fish were exported throughout the Roman empire. Judea, the southern region that spreads westward through the mountains from the Dead Sea, is craggy, dry, unfertile. But at its heart stands Jerusalem, perched on a cluster of high hills, the capital city of Israel since the time of David. Jerusalem was the seat of religious and political power, the trading center of Israel. Between Galilee of the north and Judea of the south was Samaria, a region of rough and barren land that divided Israel less geographically than ideologically.

The evangelists plot Jesus' movements on the map of Israel differently. Matthew and Luke depend heavily on Mark's account of Jesus' itinerary, but at times they too differ in particulars. John's account is strikingly different in this aspect of the Gospel story as in others. For example, in the synoptic Gospels (i.e. Mark, Matthew, and Luke), Jesus is described as going to Jerusalem only once during his public ministry. The 100-mile march from Caesarea Philippi in the extreme north to Jerusalem in the south becomes much more than a journey spanning the length of Israel. In all three of these Gospels, the journey has theological overtones. Jesus and his disciples leave their home region of Galilee, where Jesus' ministry of healing and teaching had made such impact, to start toward Jerusalem, the fateful city where Jesus, like the prophets before him, would suffer and die. Thus the journey becomes a theological odyssey during which Jesus instructs his disciples on the meaning of suffering and its consequences. John, on the other hand, has Jesus go to Jerusalem at least three times during his public ministry; the drama of a single, fateful journey is blunted.

This divergence in the four Gospel accounts is understandable when we recall the process of composition outlined in the previous chapter. The Gospel tradition did not develop as a coherent, overall story of the details of Jesus' life. The general framework was known, and individual incidents were fitted in to suit the purpose of the evangelist.

However, there is some geographical consensus that cuts across all four accounts to suggest that the historical roots of that consensus are strong. All the Gospel accounts agree that Galilee was the main arena for Jesus' public ministry. The infancy narratives of Matthew and Luke relate that Jesus was born in Bethlehem, a Judean city not far from Jerusalem. But they are quick to assert that Nazareth of Galilee became his home. Most of the incidents that take place during Jesus' ministry are also located in the north. It has been pointed out often that the lush beauty of Galilee supplied the imagery of Jesus' teaching: the sower, the birds of the air, the lilies of the field, the barns crammed with the harvest, the net filled to the breaking point. As we shall see, it was not only the rich farmland and the dominant presence of the lake that helped mold Jesus' ministry. Galilee shared in the political and religious tensions that seared Israel at the time of Jesus.

The Politics of Jesus' World

Nature had branded jagged lines across the rugged hide of Israel, but the divisions and tensions it experienced at the time of Jesus were due to realities other than geography. The period in which Jesus lived was probably one of the most tortuous in Israel's long and painful history. This too effected Jesus' ministry, and we must be aware of it.

As is so often the case, one must get a running start to appreciate any particular period in history. To appreciate first-century Palestine, one must begin with the first waves of invasion from the west, initiated by Alexander the Great.

Alexander died in 323 B.C. after having conquered most of the Mediterranean world and as far east as India. After his death, some attempt was made to consolidate these vast holdings by dividing them among his leading generals. The Middle East, including Palestine, was carved up between two generals, Seleucid and Ptolemy. These two men and their successors would dominate the political life of the Middle East for over 150 years. The Seleucid dynasty had its base in Antioch of Syria while the Ptolemies were located in Alexandria, Egypt. Israel, located in between, predictably was caught in the rivalry that soon broke out between the two competing dynasties.

For the first century of Greek occupation, Israel was ruled by the Ptolemies. Egypt was relatively far away from Palestine, so the Jews enjoyed little interference in their internal affairs. The subtle impact of Greek culture, however, was beginning to seep into Jewish thought and life. Trade and political associations with the Ptolemies in Judea necessitated contact with Greek culture and use of the Greek language. Galilee was under the rule of the Seleucids in nearby Antioch, and the incursion of Greek influence was profound. There had been some systematic colonization of the area by Greek soldiers and their families. Thus the region deserved its biblical nickname, "Galilee of the gentiles."

The bearable style of Greek occupation came to an end in 198 B.C. when all of Israel came under Seleucid rule. At first, the Seleucids allowed the province of Judea to enjoy autonomous local rule, but a thirst for increased revenues brought this experiment to an end. Then too, the specter of Rome loomed on the western horizon of the Seleucid empire. In 190 B.C., Roman naval forces dealt a crippling blow to the Greeks and exacted an enormous financial penalty as the price of defeat. To support its war effort and to make up the tribute to Rome, the Seleucids began a cruel and systematic taxation of Israel. Relations between Israel and its Greek overlords deteriorated rapidly.

Within Israel—we are speaking primarily of Judea at this point—two different sets of reactions to foreign incursion began to stir. The landed wealthy, those in positions of power, and the priestly aristocracy sought ways to accommodate their Greek overlords. But there was also a growing sentiment of resistance to oppression. The *hasidim,* or "pious ones" as many members of this group came to be called, resented the interference of the Seleucids; they considered compromise with Greek culture a threat to religious fidelity. From these two general streams of reaction would be born many of the factions that dominated the religious and political life of Jesus' own day.

The increasingly intolerable rule of the Seleucids led to one of the most extraordinary phases of post-exilic Judaism. In 167 B.C., the Seleucid ruler, Antiochus IV, tried to annex the Ptolemaic holdings in Egypt. But Roman intervention thwarted his move. Hearing of Antiochus' defeat, rebels in Judea attempted to overthrow the Greeks' puppet ruler in Jerusalem. But Antiochus, frustrated by his defeat at the hands of the Romans and embittered by the rear-guard rebellion of the Jews, sacked Jerusalem on his way back from Egypt. Worse, he desecrated the Jerusalem Temple itself: he enshrined a statue of Zeus in the Holy of Holies, the sacred inner room of the Temple where not even a devout Jew was permitted entry.

Judea erupted in revolt, led by the Hasmonean family of Mattathias and his sons. One of the sons, Judas, was nicknamed Maccabeus, "the hammer," because of his ferocious energy in opposing the gentile enemy. (The exploits of Judas and the Hasmonean family are treasured in the two biblical books of Maccabees.) By all rights, the Hasmonean revolt, however heroic, should have been no more than a suicidal gesture of resistance. Instead, the Jews won a decisive victory. By 164, the hated statue of Zeus had been cleared from the inner sanctuary, and the Temple was rededicated, an event commemorated ever since by the Jewish feast of Hanukkah. The Seleucids were unable to give their full attention to suppressing the revolt because of Roman pressure to the west and Persian threats from the east. Thus in 142, the Seleucids granted full independence to Israel, and there began almost a century of Jewish national independence, a situation never to be repeated until the modern state of Israel emerged in the middle of the 20th century.

Although freedom once again slipped away, the incredible victory of the Hasmoneans was never forgotten in

Israel. Nationalists at the time of Jesus were convinced that just as Yahweh had granted success to the Hasmoneans against the Greeks, the same victory could be achieved against the Romans. The prescription was a tragic mistake.

The Hasmonean family assumed the leadership of the new Jewish state. As courageous revolutionaries, their achievement was unparalleled; as national rulers, they proved disappointing failures, aping the worst features of the Seleucids. Even before formal independence, Jonathan Hasmonean had accepted the "gift" of the high priesthood from the Seleucid ruler, Alexander Balas. The Hasmoneans were not a priestly family, so acceptance of the gift violated hereditary accession to the high office. This pattern of expediency and compromise would typify the Hasmoneans' treatment of the priesthood throughout their reign.

Just as the *hasidim* had reacted to the incursions of the Greeks into their national and religious life, so now they found that they had much to fear from their own rulers. But the reaction was not uniform, and for the first time in Israel, the various religious and social groups operative at the time of Jesus began to take on clear definition. The Sadducees conformably found their orbit around the power base in Jerusalem. This priestly aristocracy was able to work out an accommodation with the Hasmoneans as they had with the Seleucids. Others, however, withdrew in complete revulsion from active political and religious life. Groups such as the Essenes formed monastic communes where they attempted to live with complete fidelity to the Law. Ruins of such a monastery were discovered in 1947 on the northwest shore of the Dead Sea, near the desert valley of Qumran. Included in the famous discovery was the monastery's "library" of scrolls that had been stored or hidden in caves near the main buildings. These Dead Sea Scrolls, as they have come to be known, give us a fascinating insight into the mentality of this breakaway group and an inside view of some of the religious ferment of the Hasmonean period. Groups such as at Qumran were attempting to live in utmost religious purity while awaiting the restoration of a genuine priesthood and liturgy at the defiled Jerusalem Temple.

The Pharisees were another important party that began to emerge in definite terms at this time. They steered a middle course between the compromise of the Sadducees and the radical withdrawal of the Essenes. The Pharisees refused to sell out to expediency, thus abdicating much direct involvement in the religious and political ruling circles. But their reputation among the people as strict and faithful upholders of the religious laws of Judaism made them an influential movement that had to be reckoned with.

Hasmonean abuse of power was not limited to tampering with the priesthood and the religious life of Israel. Their foreign policy became as expansionist as that of the Greeks. In the beginning, the center of the Jewish national state was the southern province of Judea. But the Hasmoneans soon began to reach out for neighboring territory. Much of the prejudice and aggravation among the various sections of the country at the time of Jesus finds its origin in this period.

Idumea, the desert territory immediately south of Judea, was quickly absorbed, and its inhabitants were forced to accept the Jewish faith. An irony of history would be that Herod and his family were Idumeans. They would form the dynasty that, with the help of Roman occupation, would replace the Hasmonean state. Herod's Idumean background meant that the authenticity of his Jewish faith would always be suspect in the eyes of most mainline Jews.

Samaria, immediately north of Judea, also was suspect. Its inhabitants had been disliked by the Judeans for many decades. The Samaritans, remnants of the northern Jewish tribes, had not been subject to the great Babylonian exile

(587-537 B.C.) as the Judeans had. As a result, much of their religious practice, and even their version of the Scriptures, differed from those of the Judeans. When the exiled Jews returned from Babylon, they refused to allow the Samaritans to participate in their national life. Thus the gulf between the two branches of Judaism widened. Suspicion and hatred of the Samaritans flamed the zeal of the Hasmonean invaders. They destroyed the Samaritan temple on Mount Gerizim and attempted—unsuccessfully—to force the Samaritans back into orthodoxy. Hatred between the two regions, already well-developed, became even more vicious. Jesus' many stories in which Samaritans appeared in a favorable light were calculated thrusts at an explosive prejudice.

Galilee too was annexed by the new state. The region's heavily gentile population was forced to accept proselytization or face deportation. Systematic programs of colonization by Jewish southerners were initiated to secure orthodoxy's foothold in the region. The campaign of judaizing Galilee seems to have had a great deal of success. By the time of Jesus, the population was mainly Jewish. But suspicion at the region's late entry into the Judean orbit, and the continuing presence of gentile inhabitants and culture, gave Galilee a demeaning reputation in the eyes of mainline Judaism. The ridiculing of Jesus' Nazorean (and thus Galilean) background at several points in the Gospels reflects this attitude.

Thus the century of independence brought about by the Hasmonean revolt rapidly became a century of deterioration and factious strife. By 63 B.C., Hasmonean excesses and the rivalry of the various groups who sought their overthrow had brought the country to the edge of civil war. Like a bemused tiger, Rome bided its time, waiting for Israel to fall. When both Sadducees and Pharisees appealed to Rome for arbitration of the power struggle, Rome not only arbitrated; it took over the entire country.

As was their policy throughout most of the empire, the

Romans preferred to administer their territories through carefully selected local rulers. By 40 B.C., the Romans had chosen a shrewd Idumean, Herod, entrusting Israel to his capable hands. Herod himself would continue in power until 4 B.C., and his sons would maintain the Herodian dynasty until almost the end of the first century A.D.

Herod the Great, as the founder of the dynasty has come to be known, gradually solidified his newly acquired kingdom with a combination of political savvy and brute terror. Herod made great efforts to ingratiate himself with his Jewish subjects, but he also had a keen taste for Greek culture. The king was a master builder. Even today, magnificent ruins of his many summer palaces and the shrines he built for some of his gentile subjects are sprinkled throughout Palestine. But the most ambitious of Herod's projects was the reconstruction of the Jerusalem Temple. The new Temple was part of Herod's calculated effort to mollify Jewish suspicions of him; it also gave an outlet to his own love of architecture. Once again, irony played its role in Jewish history. The Temple, begun in 19 B.C., was not fully completed until 63 A.D. Only seven years after its completion, it was destroyed by the Romans in the great revolt of 70 A.D. The time span of the Temple's construction meant that Jesus himself never saw its full completion. Then, too, the fact that it was Herod, an Idumean and an avowed promoter of Greek pagan culture, who had built the Temple encouraged the continued reaction of groups such as the Essenes who had withdrawn in disgust from the Jerusalem scene. These groups worshiped in protest without the benefit of the Temple liturgy, awaiting the time when Yahweh—or his Messiah—would purify the Temple and restore a legitimate priesthood.

Herod died in 4 B.C., his reputation for cunning and cruelty unabated. One story related that as he lay dying in his summer palace near Jericho, he ordered that the prominent men of the town be executed at the moment of his death to insure that sufficient mourning would coincide with his funeral. This popular estimate of Herod's cruelty is corroborated by the story in Matthew's infancy Gospel that tells of the same King's effort to liquidate a possible claimant to the throne by executing all male infants in Judea (cf. Matthew 2:16).

Herod's cruelty, however, did not negate his political ability. Despite his excesses, he was able to maintain the unity of the Hasmonean territory. At Herod's death, Rome gave the administration of Israel over to his sons. The sons of Herod, unfortunately, inherited much of their father's cruelty but little of his intelligence. The unity of the land was finished. The division of Israel and the ineptness of the Herodian dynasty encouraged the nationalist sentiment of Jesus' own day. By 67 A.D., it would break out into open and tragic revolt against Roman occupation.

The territory of Israel was now divided into three regions. This political division and the names of their rulers become the background for the Gospel story. Philip, perhaps the most sensible of the Herodians, took over the extreme northern section. He was the builder of Caesarea Philippi, the town where Peter is recorded as confessing that Jesus was the Messiah, an important turning point in the Gospel drama. Herod Antipas ruled Jesus' home region of Galilee and Perea, the area east of the Jordan river. Herod Antipas fares badly in the Gospels. Because of his illicit marriage to Herodias, wife of his half-brother Philip, he drew the fire of John the Baptist. Later, Antipas had the prophet imprisoned and executed. The ruler also showed great interest in Jesus, even fearing that he might have been John the Baptist returned from the dead. Jesus dismissed Herod's curiosity with the epithet, that "fox" (Luke 13:32). By far the most inept son of Herod was Archelaus, who was placed over the key districts of Judea, Samaria, and Idumea. Archelaus proved to be so unpopular and repressive that the Romans exiled him to France in 6 A.D. From that point on, the Romans assumed direct rule of Judea. A series of Roman prefects, under the command of the Roman legate stationed in Syria, carefully monitored Jewish life in Jerusalem. Pontius Pilate, the Roman official who would execute Jesus, was one of these prefects. This political division of the country also explains the rather complex series of events that Luke related in his account of the Passion. Pilate, as governor of Judea, had jurisdiction over the administration of Jesus' Jerusalem trial. But when he discovered that Jesus was a Galilean, he sent him to Herod Antipas, who happened to be visiting the capital city during the Jewish feast of Passover.

The division of the country under the Herodian dynasty, and the resulting tensions and frustrations it encouraged, remained the state of affairs throughout Jesus' lifetime. Under pressure of increasing taxation and political mismanagement and fired by the vision of the incredible Maccabean revolt, nationalist feelings began to build. They exploded in 67 A.D., some 30 years after the death of Jesus, when the radical Zealot party led an open rebellion against Rome. But the Romans were not the Seleucids. The revolt was crushed completely, and Jerusalem and its Temple were destroyed by 70 A.D. A suicidal attempt at a second revolt occurred in 132 A.D. with even more disastrous results. Judea was decimated by the angry Romans. Jerusalem itself was declared off limits to Jews, and the city's name was changed to Aelia Capitolina. Jewish hopes for national freedom were utterly destroyed. Only the strength of the Pharisaic party enabled Judaism to find the hope to survive.

Social and Religious Ferment

The tortuous period between the lyric hopes of Maccabean independence and the oppression of Roman occupation gives us some idea of the tense and critical times in which Jesus of Nazareth was born and carried out his mission. To gain a more complete picture of the world in which Jesus lived, let us return to the various groups and movements in the religious and social sphere of first-century Israel.

Judaism at the time of Jesus was not a monolithic block of orthodoxy. It was laced with a variety of movements and parties, and it showed considerable tolerance for diverse practice and doctrine. What united Judaism was a common religious heritage and a more-or-less common Scripture. Our knowledge of the religious patterns of Jesus' day has been increased measurably in recent years through new archaeological discoveries such as the Qumran documents. Our sources, however, are still so fragmentary that the picture must be drawn with some caution.

The Gospels themselves highlight several of the important groups of this period. We have mentioned the Sadducees, the Jerusalem-based party that drew its membership from the priestly aristocracy. This influential group was able to adapt to the political realities of Palestine, but it was much more rigid and conservative in religious matters. The Sadducees insisted that only the written Pentateuch—the first five books of the Bible, also called the Torah or the Law—should form the basis of Jewish religious life. They rejected any theological developments that sprang up in later writings or in reflection on the Law. This rigid attitude accounts for some of the Gospel disputes between the Sadducees and Jesus. In chapter 12 of Mark's Gospel, for example, we are told of a discussion about the resurrection of the dead. The Sadducees rejected the idea of resurrection because it was a relatively new theological development in Judaism. Hence their tale about the widow who had survived seven husbands was an attempt to make the resurrection appear absurd. Jesus challenged them by ignoring their question and appealing to the power of God who is able to exceed our expectations (Mark 12:27).

The Sadducee party did not survive the catastrophes of

70 and 132 A.D. Once the Temple had been destroyed and their base of power in Jerusalem dispersed, the Sadducees do not seem to have had the resilience necessary to continue their role in Judaism's critical new situation.

No Jewish group dominates the pages of the Gospels as much as the Pharisees. The image they acquire in the Gospels is uniformly negative; however, we should accept this stereotype with a great deal of caution. The name "Pharisee" probably derives from the Hebrew word meaning "to separate," referring to the strict adherence to Law that characterized their way of life and distinguished them from less faithful elements in Judaism. The Pharisaic movement found its origin in the *hasidim* reaction to the excesses of the Hasmoneans and the puppets of Greek rule before them. Their faithful adherence to the Mosaic Law and their rejection of compromise with foreign influence earned them great respect and influence among the Jews.

Pharisaic devotion to the Law should not be seen as a blind embrace of legalism. Their extensive system of oral commentary on the Law and its detailed prescriptions was an attempt to make the Law livable, not impossible. For example, the Law might command rest on the Sabbath; but how could one know if he or she were faithful to this command? The Pharisaic commentaries and prescriptions were designed to give precise guidance for every possible contingency: how far one might walk, how much to eat, what sort of movement was permitted, and so on. Thus the Pharisees, unlike the Sadducees, were open to new development in Jewish thought. For them, the great network of oral commentary that had grown up around the Law in the rabbinic schools of Israel was not a subversion of the Law but an insurance that it was living and active.

The inner strength of the Pharisaic movement and its basis of power in the synagogue rather than the Temple helped assure its leadership role in the chaotic period following the Jewish revolts. It was the Pharisees who effectively reorganized Jewish religious life and lifted it from the ashes. Although the Temple was gone, the Law remained. If the sacred rituals of the sacrifices at Jerusalem had ceased, one could still worship God with a clean heart by strict fidelity to his commands. Jewish national independence might lay shattered in the ruins of the Zealot revolt, but the messianic hopes of Israel could survive even this purification. Thus the Pharisees left their stamp on the character of post-70 Judaism, a character that would remain indelible for centuries: Modern Judaism is derived from Pharisaism.

The prominence of the Pharisaic party in Judaism during the period when the Gospels were being written helps explain some of the uniformly negative image that appears in the Gospels. Jesus himself undoubtedly had fundamental differences with the Pharisees over interpretation of the Law and even more basic differences about the nature of religious fidelity. It is likely too that the Pharisees' zeal for the Law could lead to an excess of legalism and to a concern for externals bordering on hypocrisy. Thus the Gospels' indictment of the Pharisees cannot be completely overturned. But it is a Christian responsibility to be aware of the complexity of the picture lest the Gospel critique of the Pharisees become an excuse for anti-Semitism and anti-Judaism, as it often has been in the past. In other words, the historical situation through which the Gospel tradition passed, prior to and during its inclusion in the written Gospels, accounts for much of the negative tone regarding these Jewish leaders. In the book of Acts, we read that many of the Pharisees actually joined the early Christian community. St. Paul boasted of being a Pharisee. But by the time the Gospels were written, they had become a symbol of opposition to Jesus and prime instigators of his death. The change is due in part to the fact that the early Christian church and orthodox Judaism had drifted further and further apart, especially after the crisis of 70 A.D. One result of Jewish effort to rebuild was a lessening of tolerance for fringe groups within Judaism.

The leadership of the Pharisees gradually imposed a tighter orthodoxy on Jewish life, based on strict fidelity to the Law. Christian critique of the Law and the church's openness to gentile converts put the early community on a collision course with Judaism. The fact that the Jews generally did not accept the Gospel and the efforts of some Jews to thwart the Christian mission led to a fratricidal bitterness that should not be overlooked when we assess the Gospel portrait of the Pharisees. Certainly some of this tension and polemic helped reduce their image in the Gospel story to that of mere opponents and persecutors of Jesus.

To acknowledge the role that later history played in the Gospel portrait of the Pharisees does not subvert the Gospels' reliability; but once again it urges that we read the accounts with full understanding of the process that produced them.

Our review of Jewish history uncovers other groups in the Judaism, even though some of them play only minor roles in the Gospel story. The Essenes, as noted, were a group that reacted in radical fashion to the compromises of official religious life under the Hasmoneans. They withdrew from ordinary life to set up communes where fidelity to the Law could be carried out in monastic isolation. The Essenes are not mentioned in the Gospel. John the Baptist's insistence on ritual washing as a sign of repentence and his preaching of an imminent judgment echo Essene practice and doctrine. Some commentators suggest that his desert sojourn prior to his public ministry may have been spent in contact with a group such as that at Qumran. But there is no direct evidence in the Gospel. During the revolt of 67-70 A.D., the Romans destroyed the monastery of Qumran. The Essenian movement seems to have died out, unable to find a place in the adjustment of Jewish life called for by the crisis of 70.

Another group without credits in the Gospel—but of vital importance for the fate of Judaism—was the Zealots.

They emerge clearly as a movement or party at the time of the first revolt against Rome in 70 A.D. But it is likely that their brand of radical nationalism already had begun to crystallize during Jesus' own lifetime. The Zealots maintained that Jewish independence could be achieved only by military action against the Romans. The brawn of the occupying power did not discourage the Zealots; they firmly believed that Yahweh himself would intervene to establish the Kingdom of Israel, if his faithful servants would only begin the struggle. The Zealots took heart from the incredible victory of the Hasmoneans: What God had done to the Seleucids, he could do to the Romans.

The only possible reference to the Zealots in the Gospels is the mention that Simon "Zelotes" was one of the Apostles. Many scholars believe that Simon may have been a member of the Zealot movement before joining the ranks of Jesus' disciples. Jesus' preaching of the imminent coming of the Kingdom and the force of his leadership easily could have attracted the Zealots. Here perhaps was someone who could galvanize the masses and begin the struggle against Rome. The Roman authorities themselves might have feared this possibility, thus justifying their summary execution of Jesus for his claim to be "King of the Jews." But an examination of Jesus' teaching shows that he carefully distanced himself from the Zealot movement on such questions as Roman taxation and the use of violence. The image of Jesus as a political revolutionary finds little support in the Gospels.

The Zealots eventually brought off their revolution. A series of abortive attempts to overthrow the Romans had marked the early decades of the first century. But a general uprising, under Zealot leadership, was not triggered until 66 A.D. It was snuffed out by the Romans by 70 A.D. The Zealot survivors fled to the rock fortress of Herod at Masada, a sheer, flat-top mountain on the southwestern shore of the Dead Sea. The Zealots held out for nearly three years while the Romans besieged the fortress. When they realized their cause was hopeless, the revolutionaries committed mass suicide rather than submit to Roman slavery. Sixty years later, another rebellion was attempted, but Roman might could not be overcome, and the Zealots' cause was doomed.

Not all or even most of the Jewish people living at the time of Jesus can be fitted into the few categories we have catalogued. The historian Josephus, a contemporary of this period, suggests that the Pharisees never numbered more than 35,000. His figures may be questioned, but it is likely that these parties and movements never formed a majority of the people. Most of the Jews of Jesus' time were the ordinary, uninfluential people who make up the life of any country in any period. Israel was basically agrarian, and the bulk of the population were peasants, coaxing a living from the reluctant soil that covered most of Palestine. Shepherds were still numerous among a people whose ancesters were nomads. The fishermen of Galilee, from whom Jesus selected many of his disciples, were relatively prosperous, owning boats and having access to the rich fisheries of the Lake. There were a few sizable cities in Palestine: Jerusalem, of course, and the heavily gentile Tiberias in Galilee and coastal cities such as Caesarea, Tyre and Sidon where the urban masses—tradesmen, merchants, the professional classes—made their homes.

The political tensions that rankled Israel at this time were compounded by other problems. The burden of taxation, particularly for the peasant, was almost unbearable. The upkeep of the Temple and its worship traditionally demanded a tithe of the male Jew. Added to this were the inexorable demands of Roman taxation, which itself invited abuse. Hired Jewish agents were given a quota to fulfill, and they were practically free to levy taxes as they saw fit. The tax collector was understandably despised both as a Roman quisling and as a thief. Some historians estimate that the taxation of the Galilean peasant may have reached as much as 40 percent. In addition, much of the land was in the hands of absentee owners, especially in the north. There was little opportunity for redress and no satisfaction in one's accomplishments.

The pressure of injustice was matched for many of these people by a burden of religious guilt. The Pharisees had spelled out the conditions for righteousness under the Law, and they were respected for their scrupulous fidelity. But, for most of the people, such fidelity was impossible. Those whose occupations brought them into contact with gentiles were proscribed as officially unclean or incapable of keeping the Law: shopkeepers, toll collectors, traders, and so on. Others, like the shepherds, bore the stigma of popular suspicion for dishonesty, much like the Gypsies of modern Europe. Too, these groups found that such suspicions banned them from Temple worship and from being able to give testimony at a court of law. And, of course, public sinners, such as prostitutes and other outcasts, had absolutely no hope of achieving fidelity under the Law. Thus for many of the common citizens of Israel—the *amharetz* or "people of the land"—the way to religious fidelity was clear; but often too that way was permanently sealed.

Such was the world of Jesus. There is much that we do not know. The historical records that give us a glimpse into this past are fragmentary. But what we do know is helpful. The world of Jesus was a cosmopolitan world, in touch with both Greek and Roman cultures. An educated man might even be tri-lingual, fluent not only in his native Aramaic but able to carry on business in Greek and Latin. It was also a world of deep religious conviction, where dissent and individual persuasion were generally tolerated. But it was also a world of ominous political tension, a world that seemed to be moving toward an inevitable holocaust, a world in which the birthright of God's people had been diminished by oppression and despair.

This was the world that Jesus of Nazareth ministered to. The later world in which the Gospels were written experienced profound changes separating it from the time and conditions that Jesus faced. Judaism was profoundly transformed, and the Christian mission was moving across the face of the empire. But the Gospel tradition and the words and works of Jesus it portrays still find roots in this past world. To know of it is to know something more about Jesus.

Chapter 3

Jesus and His Own

Human experience tells us that we are revealed by our relationships: the friends we make, the people we reach out to, the way we respond to those who approach us. The kind of persons we are is reflected too in the reactions of those who know us. It had to be the same with Jesus. He was not isolated from the ordinary network of social relationships that make up any human life. People observed him, were drawn to him, loved him; some rejected him. These types of reactions, as spelled out in the Gospels, are an important source for our portrait of Jesus.

But once again, the nature of the Gospel material cautions us to evaluate it on its own terms. The evangelists and the traditions they used made no attempt to give us a psychological profile of Jesus. In fact, such interest probably would have seemed a strange curiosity to citizens of the first century. The material in the Gospels was chosen primarily for what it had to say about the meaning of Christian life. Almost everything said about Jesus in the Gospels ultimately is a statement about what a Christian is to be. This fact does not bankrupt our attempt to learn about Jesus from his relationships; it simply persuades us to draw our conclusions carefully.

Before we begin to examine Gospel material that deals with Jesus and his relationships, we should give some attention to the theme that was the starting point for practically everything that Jesus said or did: the Kingdom of God. Most of the friends and enemies that Jesus makes in the Gospels are related to his zeal for the Kingdom. This is not to say that Jesus was rigidly functional in his dealings with people. Rather, Jesus' ministry of the Kingdom was the basis upon which the Gospel tradition itself selected the material we have.

Jesus and the Kingdom

Every New Testament scholar would agree that the central theme of Jesus' ministry was the "Kingdom of God." Under this program can be gathered a large percentage of his individual sayings, his most eloquent parables, and the purpose of the healing and teaching ministry he undertook. Mark and Matthew explicity state that Jesus' inaugural preaching announced the coming of the Kingdom (cf. Mark 1:14-15; Matthew 4:17). An important Kingdom text from Isaiah 61 forms the keynote in Luke's account of the beginning of Jesus' ministry in Nazareth (4:14-30).

The Kingdom of God was not an invention of Jesus or the Gospels. The theme had deep roots in Israel's religious history. Old Testament religion basically was a religion of hope, of an unshakable confidence that Yahweh eventually would vindicate his people and bestow on them the blessings of peace, prosperity, and fullness of life. There are several theological symbols or themes that expressed this fundamental Jewish faith. Yahweh's rescue of his people from slavery in Egypt, for example, became the basis of hope for a future, definitive rescue from sin and oppression. His promise of the land was elevated to a future hope in Israel's freedom from threat and domination. Even the act of creation itself became a theological symbol of an ultimate redemption that would bring about a new act of life-giving mercy. Thus Israel's hope for a future Kingdom of God became one of several religious themes that expressed the unshakable trust of the Jew that Yahweh was faithful.

As with many Old Testament themes, this future hope was rooted in the historic past. The notion of the Kingdom of God was rooted in Israel's own experience of monarchy. The Jewish people adopted a monarchical form of government only gradually and with some hesitation. As the Jewish tribes consolidated their conquests of Palestine, they were content with a loose confederation under the leadership of judges or local tribal officers. Yahweh alone was king over Israel, and no human would dare to usurp this role in a theocratic state. But as need for a tighter social organization asserted itself and as Israel saw the appeal of surrounding cultures, it too turned towards monarchy. Their spokesmen stoutly maintained that Yahweh alone was king, and the earthly ruler was only his vicegerent. But in fact, Israel had a king: Saul, David, Solomon, and a long line that would continue for centuries. David, certainly the most celebrated of the Jewish kings, consolidated the monarchical system and established Jerusalem as the center of government and worship.

Israel's experience of monarchy was not satisfying. David and Solomon were flashes of brilliance in a long line of often mediocre and sometimes corrupt rulers. Almost constant interference from foreign powers complicated matters. Finally, the monarchy was snuffed out by the invasion of the Babylonians in 587 B.C. Zedekiah, last of the Judean kings, died in exile.

The Davidic monarchy was never restored as a political structure, but it did become the basis of a fervent religious hope. The Kingdom, it was believed, would appear once more, but this time not as a symbol of human ambition. Yahweh himself would make clear that he alone was king, not only over Israel but over all the earth. Thus the religious concept of the Kingdom of God did not refer to some heavenly Camelot. It was not a kingdom in any sort of spatial or local sense. It referred, rather, to God's reigning in power so that all could know and experience his might.

The Kingdom was not to be a state of bliss carefully constructed by men. It would not be the result of the gradual evolution of an enlightened society. The emphasis of the Kingdom of God theme was not that men would draw near to God but that God would draw near to men. God himself would establish the kind of world that manifested his mercy and justice, a world where hostility and infidelity would cease. In the evocative words of Isaiah 11:6-9, it would be a world where:

the wolf shall be a guest of the lamb, and the leopard shall lie down with the kid; the calf and the young lion shall browse together, with a little child to guide them. The cow and the bear shall be neighbors, together their young shall rest; the lion shall eat hay like the ox. The baby shall play by the cobra's den, and the child lay his hand on the adder's lair. There shall be no harm or ruin on all my holy mountain; for the earth shall be filled with knowledge of the Lord, as waters cover the sea.

Jesus was a Jew who shared the longings and hopes of his people. He drew on the rich theme of the Kingdom of God as a way of understanding his own vocation and ministry. The uniqueness of Jesus' preaching of the Kingdom was not so much the way he defined it but the emphasis he gave to it. In the Judaism of Jesus' day, the theme had not been given particular attention. The Pharisees, for example, spoke of "taking upon oneself the yoke of God's Kingdom"; but this referred to total obedience to the Law and to the one God whose will the Law expressed. They did not emphasize the Kingdom as an imminent reality in the way that Jesus did. The same is true of the Essenes; the concept of the Kingdom does not figure prominently in the writings of the Dead Sea Scrolls. Only the Zealots utilized this concept; but for them, the Kingdom was to be achieved by overt political action on the part of men. Thus the religious concept received a twist very much different from the emphasis of Jesus. For

Jesus, the Kingdom was the work of God. And everything that Jesus said or did was evidence that the Kingdom was beginning to break into the world. His acts of healing and compassion, his words of wisdom, were all directed toward creating the kind of life that would characterize the Kingdom over which Yahweh himself would be master. We will return to this point repeatedly as we search out the Gospel portrait of Jesus. For the moment, let us concentrate on how Jesus' ministry of the Kingdom focuses on the people he chose to be with.

Jesus and His Disciples

One of the most touching and revealing aspects of the Gospel story is that of Jesus in the company of his disciples. They are an almost constant presence, gaping in awe at his acts of power. They are confidants of his most important teaching, shuffling along at his side as his mission drove him through the crowds of Galilee. We learn much about Jesus in considering his followers.

All of the Gospels relate that one of the first things Jesus did was to gather disciples. Mark (1:16-20) states that as soon as Jesus began his public ministry in Galilee, he recruited Simon, his brother Andrew, and Zebedee's two sons, James and John. Matthew's account is the same (4:18-22). As Jesus' ministry progressed, more would join him. In Luke (5:1-11), the formal call of the first disciples came somewhat after Jesus' ministry had picked up momentum; but the cure of Simon's mother-in-law (4:38-39) indicates that Luke too was aware that the calling of disciples was one of Jesus' first priorities. In John's Gospel, some of the Baptist's own disciples were attracted to Jesus immediately after his baptism (1:35-51).

By gathering disciples, Jesus again showed that he was a man of his time. It was common practice among the rabbis, or teachers, of Jesus' day to attract followers or disciples. But there are several unique features of Gospel discipleship that must not be overlooked.

The disciple-master relationship is rare in the Old Testament. The practice probably resulted from Greek influence in Palestine. The method of learning in which a pupil developed a strong personal bond with a teacher or master was characteristic of the Greek philosophical schools. The ideal of the disciple was to choose a master teacher from whom one could learn genuine wisdom. In a Jewish context, this meant choosing a rabbi in order to learn the delicate art of interpreting the Law. The disciple subordinated himself to the master, learning from him, serving him. By constant repetition and association, the master handed on to his disciples the heritage of the past and the skill to interpret it. Discipleship, however, was not a permanent status. The goal of learning was that the disciple himself would be trained to be master, no longer dependent on his rabbi once he had absorbed the teacher's wisdom.

But discipleship on Jesus' terms was quite different. First, one did not become a disciple of Jesus by choice but through a "call." The Gospel stories that relate this are undoubtedly sterotyped, trimmed to the essential details in order to make their point. The process that drew the disciples to Jesus was probably more extensive and built on a developing relationship to him. But the "call" stories in their clipped form emphasize that it was upon Jesus' initiative that the disciples were drawn into his mission. Simon, later called Peter, and his brother Andrew are casting a fishing net into the lake when Jesus walks into their life with commanding sovereignty: "Come after me and I will make you fishers of men." The response is unhesitating: "They immediately abandoned their nets and became his followers" (Matthew 1:20). James and John are working on their boats with their father Zebedee. Jesus calls, and "they immediately abandoned boat and father to follow him" (Matthew 1:22). Levi sits at his tax collector's post. "Follow me" is the sovereign call, and, the Gospel simply notes, "Levi got up and followed him" (Matthew

9:9-10). In John's account, the early disciples are fascinated by Jesus and begin to follow him. They inquire of Jesus where he lives. The response is blunt: "Come and see" (1:39).

The call to discipleship cuts through the ordinary ways of life, whether "clean" or "unclean," whether fishermen or hated tax collector. The response is expected to be instant, complete, unquestioned. It is obvious that, as always, the Gospel accounts have one eye on Christian life and commitment. The reaction of the disciples models what the response of each Christian is to be to the Gospel. Nevertheless, the power of Jesus' personality and his ability to summon strong allegiance are the obvious basis for this "call" tradition.

The Gospel portrayal of discipleship is also distinctive by the fact that the call is not simply to learn a body of doctrine or the skills of interpretation from a master. It is, instead, a call to a relationship with Jesus that never ceases. The disciple is not expected to "graduate" or to outgrow his need to follow Jesus. "As to you, avoid the title 'Rabbi.' One among you is your teacher, the rest are learners . . . Avoid being called teachers. Only one is your teacher, the Messiah" (Matthew 23:8-10). The text, from the highly polemical chapter 23 of Matthew's Gospel, no doubt reflects the growing rift between the early church and Pharisaism. But its insistence on the permanent nature of Christian discipleship accords with the entire Gospel story.

The bond between Jesus and his disciples is sealed by their share in his mission. It is here perhaps that the distinctive aspects of Christian discipleship stand out most clearly. The disciples are called not simply to be with Jesus but to observe what he does, to learn from him, so that they might share in his work for the Kingdom. From the very beginning of the Gospel story, the disciples are the privileged witnesses of the healing activity of Jesus. To them he directs his parables and his most important teaching. They are called to share his style of life, even to share his suffering and hardship.

A clear indication of this is found in chapter 8 of Matthew's Gospel. Jesus and his followers are about to get into boats to cross over the lake. The evangelist uses the situation to illustrate forcefully the demands of discipleship on Jesus' terms. As the group is about to embark, a scribe, a Jew well-versed in the Law, comes forward: "Teacher, wherever you go I will come after you." Jesus' reply is sobering: "The foxes have lairs, the birds in the sky have nests, but the Son of Man has nowhere to lay his head." Another person, already a disciple, also speaks: "Lord, let me go and bury my father first." What request could be more reasonable? But the reply of Jesus refuses to acknowledge any priority above that of devotion to the work of the Kingdom: "Follow me and let the dead bury the dead." The scene closes with this observation: "He got into the boat and his disciples followed him" (Matthew 8:18-23). The entire incident underlines the uniqueness of discipleship with Jesus. It is a call to share in his mission, including its hardships, and it is a call that brooks allegiance to no other priority.

Thus the presence of the disciples as witnesses to Jesus' ministry signals that they too will share in this work. Each of the Gospels explicitly makes this point. The same purpose and power that describe the ministry of Jesus are assigned to the mission of the disciples. What Jesus does in his healing and teaching ministry, so must the disciples do. In Mark 6:12f., for instance, after the evangelist has spent several chapters describing the ministry of Jesus, the disciples are sent off to do the same sort of marvelous activities: "preaching the need of repentance . . . expelled many demons . . . anointed the sick with oil, and worked many cures." Matthew's construction of the mission instructions in chapter 10 of his Gospel is even more explicit: "As you go, make this announcement: 'The reign of God is at hand!' Cure the sick, raise the dead, heal the leprous, expel demons. The gift you have received, give as a gift" (10:7-8). The mission of the Twelve in Luke 9:1ff. is similar: "Jesus now called the Twelve together and gave them power and authority to overcome all demons and to cure diseases. He sent them forth to proclaim the reign of God and to heal the afflicted." John's Gospel has no mission "discourse" as the other three do; but the climactic scene of chapter 20 stresses the same equation between the mission of Jesus and that of his disciples: "As the Father has sent me, so I send you" (20:21).

The Gospels make clear, then, that the strong bond of fellowship between Jesus and his disciples was built not only on the force of his presence that called them to him, nor simply on their affection for and trust in him, but on the fact that he shared with them his own vision of life and the ministry that expressed it. There are touching bits of evidence in the Gospel that spin off from the disciples' pride in their association with Jesus. They become protective, attempting to shield Jesus from the eager crowds (Mark 10:13). They are jealous of the power that their common sense of mission gives them, and they resent the outsider who attempts to imitate them (Luke 9:40). They become familiar with Jesus and speak with democratic bluntness: "Teacher, does it not matter to you that we are going to drown?" (Mark 4:38). "Are we to go and spend two hundred days' wages for bread to feed a crowd like this!" (Mark 6:37). "You can see how this crowd hems you in, yet you ask, 'Who touched me?' " (Mark 5:31). They begin to sense too the risk their mission entails, and they remind Jesus of their commitment to him: "We have put aside everything to follow you!" (Mark 10:28). "Lord, to whom shall we go? You have the words of eternal life. We have come to believe; we are convinced that you are God's Holy One" (John 6:68).

Thus the position of the disciples is, in Christian perspective, awesome. They walk with Jesus. They enjoy his trust and affection. They share in his mission and are equipped with the power to accomplish it. But to picture the disciples of Jesus solely in such well-groomed terms does not do justice to the Gospel presentation. The disciples do not come off as recruitment-poster models —flawless, handsome, bigger than life. In fact, one of the most amazing aspects of the Gospel story is that it avoids building the disciples into bronzed heroes. Any attempt to idealize them would have been understandable. After all, these were the first to be chosen by Jesus. These were the men who formed the earliest Christian community and transmitted the teaching of Jesus to later generations of believers. To idealize is the natural tendency of any community tradition. But the disciples of Jesus are far short of ideal. One can conclude only that the facts of the matter were too glaring and too instructive for later generations of Christians to gloss over.

First, the very origin of the disciples causes notice. What sort of men did Jesus choose to join in his mission? Snappy, intelligent lieutenants who quickly sensed the genius of what their leader was about and then efficiently and enthusiastically joined in? Were they eager to assume responsibility in a mission of crucial importance? The Gospels are unanimous in declaring that things were not this way. The call stories themselves list men of prosaic background: fishermen and a tax collector. Two of them are nicknamed *Boanerges*, "hotheads" (literally, "sons of thunder"). One apparently is a former Zealot. Each time the Gospels list the chosen Twelve, the most intimate of Jesus' disciples, they grimly mention Judas "who would betray him." There is no indication from the Gospel story or from its citation of the disciples' background that they were well-educated or even so inclined. And nothing in the Gospel story suggests a quick conversion in that direction.

But the Gospels do more than leave the reader with an impression of the disciples as "ordinary." One of the consistent features of the disciples was a chronic dullness.

They exhibit an embarrassing inability to understand who Jesus is or what he is about. The Gospel of Mark emphasizes this trait of the disciples more than any other Gospel. As do the other evangelists, he puts the disciples in a privileged position. They witness Jesus' miracles, they are exposed to his teaching. Yet they seem unable to comprehend any of these awesome events.

Mark's Gospel shows Jesus amazed that his disciples are baffled by the parables: "You do not understand this parable? How then are you going to understand other figures like it?" (4:13). Jesus chides them for their lack of faith when they fail to recognize the significance of his power over the forces of nature: "Why are you so terrified? Why are you lacking in faith?" (4:39). The same lack of comprehension marks their reaction to the great messianic signs of the multiplication of the loaves and the walking on the water: "They were taken aback by these happenings, for they had not understood about the loaves. On the contrary, their minds were completely closed to the meaning of the events" (6:51-52). Jesus seems to blurt out his exasperation at the dullness of his followers as his public ministry nears its finale: " 'Do you still not see or comprehend? Are your minds completely blinded? Have you eyes but no sight? Ears but no hearing? Do you remember when I broke the five loaves for the five thousand, how many baskets of fragments you gathered up?' They answered, 'Twelve.' 'When I broke the seven loaves for the four thousand, how many full hampers of fragments did you collect?' They answered, 'Seven.' He said to them again, 'Do you still not understand?' " (8:17-21).

In Mark's Gospel, even what might seem like the disciples' better moments become clouded with misunderstanding. Peter proclaims that Jesus is the "Messiah" (8:29), but the subsequent dialogue reveals that Peter interprets this title in a way that Jesus cannot accept. Peter's expectations are similar to those of many of his countrymen of first-century Palestine. The Messiah would be a mighty leader who would restore Israel's former glory, and he would lift away the yoke of political oppression. Jesus' immediate reference to suffering and death clashes with Peter's vision of power. He takes his Master aside to chide him as one might a foolish child. Jesus' words are an incredible indictment of the leader of the disciples: "Get out of my sight, you satan! You are not judging by God's standards but by man's" (Mark 8:33).

The zest for power that infects Peter is contagious. The disciples begin to sense the potential of Jesus' forceful leadership and his impact on the crowds. Symptoms of a growing ambition mark the long journey from Caesarea Philippi in the north to Jerusalem in the south (in Mark cf. 8:27-10:52). Whenever Jesus warns his disciples of the suffering and hardship bound up with his mission of selfless service, they respond with uncomprehending ambition. On the road they argue about "who was the most important" (9:34). Zebedee's sons, James and John, sidle up to Jesus in an attempt to gain positions of importance when their Master takes over rule of Israel (10:35-36). Jesus' reply is blunt with eloquence: "You do not know what you are asking." The other 10 are not exempt from the blunder of James and John; they become indignant at their maneuver. Jesus calls them all together to try to break through their incomprehension: "You know how among the Gentiles those who seem to exercise authority lord it over them; their great ones make their importance felt. It cannot be like that with you. Anyone among you who aspires to greatness must serve the rest; whoever wants to rank first among you must serve the needs of all. The Son of Man has not come to be served but to serve—to give his life in ransom for the many" (10:42-45).

There is little doubt that Mark's emphasis on the failures of the disciples is part of his "Gospel program." The grim account of ambition and misunderstanding serves as a challenge to discipleship abuse in Mark's own church.

Any Christian who thirsts for power, or who fails to realize that suffering is the lot of anyone called to serve, could find himself mirrored in the response of Jesus' disciples. Jesus' rebuke to his followers is directed now to the Christians of Mark's church.

The same fundamental portrait of the disciples in the other Gospels indicates that Mark's emphasis is only that: an emphasis not a fabrication. The other evangelists back off somewhat from the unrelieved grimness of Mark's account, but the disciples never reach hero status. Matthew, for instance, hesitates to indict the disciples for "lacking faith" (cf. Mark 4:40). But his own characterization of them, "men of little faith," remains far short of sainthood (Matthew 8:26). Luke seems to deal more gently with the disciples, but even in his account the catalogue of failure and dullness is not absent. In John, the disciples do not fully perceive who Jesus is or what his words mean until after the resurrection (cf. John 14:26; 15:26; 16:4; 16:12-14).

The strongest Gospel indictment of the disciples is not for their lack of comprehension but for their ultimate failure of Jesus. Again, the presence of such a disappointing account of the disciples in the tradition testifies to its foundation in history. The Gospels state that Jesus' disciples desert him at the crisis of arrest and impending death. Again, the reaction of the evangelists is different, but their basic agreement is testimony to the strength of the tradition.

All three of the synoptics present the disciples as sleeping during the ordeal of Jesus' prayer in the garden, although Luke appears to soften their failure by noting that they were "exhausted with grief" (22:45). Mark and Matthew bluntly state that, at the very moment of the arrest, all of his disciples "deserted him and fled" (cf. Mark 14:50; Matthew 26:56). Luke passes over the moment in silence, but the absence of the disciples in the Passion story shows he has no tradition contrary to Mark and

Matthew. In John, it is Jesus himself who secures the release of the disciples from the arrest party (18:8). But in all four Gospel accounts, Jesus faces the dark hours of his suffering and death utterly alone. Only two disciples stand out from the shadows of that gloom: Judas who betrays him for 30 pieces of silver and leads the armed band to the garden; Peter, the leader of the disciples, who denies his discipleship when a servant girl associates him with Jesus the Galilean. John alone notes that "the beloved disciple," that mysterious figure who plays a witness role in the fourth Gospel, stood with the Mother of Jesus near the cross as Jesus dies (19:26).

The Gospels' last word on the disciples is not their failure but their reconciliation with Jesus. In a true sense, the Gospel story of the resurrection is a story of reconciliation. Just as Jesus of Nazareth originally had summoned the disciples from their former way of life to become his disciples, now, after the resurrection, the Risen Lord takes the initiative to restore the broken bond between himself and the disciples. In the synoptic Gospels, the promise of reconciliation already had been made at the Last Supper. The evangelists heighten the awareness of the disciples' failure by having Jesus predict his betrayal by Judas and his desertion by the others in a setting of table fellowship. But along with this prediction comes a promise: "After I am raised up, I will go to Galilee ahead of you" (Mark 14:28; Matthew 26:32). Luke once again dampens the disciples' negative image, but Jesus does state: "Simon, Simon! Remember that Satan has asked for you, to sift you all like wheat. But I have prayed for you that your faith may never fail. You in turn must strengthen your brothers" (Luke 22:31-32).

This promise of reconciliation lays the foundations for the resurrection appearances of Jesus. In Mark 16:6, the women who come to the tomb to anoint Jesus discover that he is not to be found among the dead. The angel repeats Jesus' Last Supper promise: "Go now and tell his disciples and Peter, 'He is going ahead of you to Galilee, where you will see him just as he told you.' " In Matthew's account (cf. 28:7), the angel repeats the same message. But the promise of reconciliation is stated even more explicitly by the Risen Lord himself as he appears to the women on their way back from the empty tomb: "Go and carry the news to my brothers that they are to go to Galilee, where they will see me" (Matthew 28:10). The predicted reunion becomes the majestic finale of the Gospel. "Those who had entertained doubts fell down in homage" (28:17). Jesus responds by commissioning his disciples to carry on his ministry throughout the whole world, until the end of time.

Luke conveys the same sort of message through the hauntingly beautiful Emmaus story. Two of Jesus' disillusioned disciples leave Jerusalem and the company of the other disciples; they believe that their cause is finished. The Risen Lord himself—unrecognized—joins them and explains the meaning of his suffering. They recognize him at last in "the breaking of the bread" (24:35). Their confidence restored, they turn back to join the community of believers in Jerusalem. Luke too concludes his Gospel with a scene of reunion. The Risen Lord breaks into the isolation of the upper room and offers a greeting of "peace" to the disciples gathered there. Their panic is transformed into ecstasy when they recognize that it is Jesus. Again, reconciliation takes the form of a commission. In the name of Jesus, penance for the remission of sins is to be preached to all the nations, beginning at Jerusalem. "You are the witnesses of this" (27:48).

John's Gospel also draws to a close in a mood of reconciliation and restoration. Jesus suddenly appears in the room where the disciples are huddled in fear. Once more, "peace" is his greeting. The recommissioned disciples are sent "as the Father has sent me" (20:21), and they are given the gift of the Holy Spirit (20:22).

It is not possible to harmonize the resurrection accounts

of the four Gospels. Here, more than any other place in the Gospel story, each evangelist goes his own way to muster the traditions to suit the purpose of his Gospel account. But one theme binds the traditions together: The experience of the resurrection was one of reconciliation. Their share in the ministry of the Kingdom, forfeited by their desertion, is restored to the disciples through the Risen Lord's own initiative.

Thus the Gospel image of the disciples is complex, fascinating, decidedly human. Perhaps Peter stands out as the clearest illustration of the disciple. He has a major role in all four accounts, and he became the acknowledged leader of the early church. But Peter's prominence in Christian history did not earn him immunity from the sober eye of the Gospel tradition. His accomplishments and his failures share the spotlight. He is the first called in all the accounts (Matthew 4:18; Mark 1:16; Luke 5:10). He becomes the disciples' leader and their natural spokesman (Mark 8:29, etc.). He is the chosen witness of Jesus' most dramatic signs of power (e.g. the Transfiguration, cf. Mark 9:2). He alone confesses that Jesus is the Messiah. He is the prime witness of the resurrection, listed first in all of the traditional lists (cf. Paul's citation of this tradition in 1 Corinthians 15:5). He alone is given an explicit role of leadership in the new community (cf. Matthew 16:18-19; Luke 22:31-32; John 21:15 ff.). But his flaws are equally prominent. He is impetuous and thickheaded. His recognition of Jesus as Messiah is soured by a misunderstanding of what messiahship means (cf. Mark 8:32). Jesus himself called Peter "Satan" (Mark 8:33) and an "obstacle" to Jesus' intended mission (Matthew 16:23). If the other disciples are guilty of desertion, Peter compounds his fall by false bravado (Mark 14:29, etc.) and, worst of all, by a cowardly denial of his Master (Mark 14:66-72, etc.).

But the evangelists are quick to stress that if Peter's failure was the most glaring, Jesus' reconciliation with him is the most firm. Even at the moment of denial, the synoptic Gospels prepare for Peter's restoration to discipleship. In Mark (14:72) and Matthew (26:75), the chilling cockcrow reminds Peter of Jesus' prediction during the supper. His sworn denials cease, and Peter sobs with remorse. Luke heightens the drama: Peter's remorse is triggered not simply by the signal of a cockcrow but by having Jesus himself turn to face the disciple who repeatedly has denied that he even knew Jesus (22:61). John terminates the account of the denial without any indication of Peter's reaction; but in a resurrection appearance by the Lake of Galilee, the Risen Lord heals the wounds of Peter's triple denial by drawing from him a touching threefold affirmation of love (21:15-17). And Peter's prominence in all of the resurrection tradition testifies to his complete restoration to leadership in the early community.

Perhaps the most striking Petrine vignette in all of the Gospels is found in chapter 14 of Matthew, a Gospel that gives more attention to Peter than the other evangelists do. The story of Jesus walking on the sea makes a single, vivid picture of what discipleship means. As in several of the Gospel nature miracles, the scene underlines the divine power of Jesus. Like Yahweh in many of the Old Testament psalms, the Messiah reveals his power by overcoming the chaos of an angry sea. But in Matthew's account of this incident, emphasis falls as well on Peter and the disciples. Matthew adds to the account of Mark (cf. Mark 6:45-52) the section where Peter, heartened by his recognition of the Lord (Matthew 14:28), asks to share in Jesus' awesome power. Amazingly, he is able to duplicate Jesus' mastery over the powers of nature. But, then, sensing the threat of wind and sea, Peter's faith becomes crippled by fear and doubt; he begins to sink. Only a desperate prayer (14:30) rescues him: "Lord, save me!" The Gospel notes the instant response: "Jesus at once stretched out his hand and caught him" (14:31). The words of Jesus echo the Matthean image of the disciples: "How little faith you have! Why did you falter?'' The rest of the disciples, who witness this episode, fall down in worship before Jesus; they utter one of the strongest confessions of faith in the Gospel: "Beyond doubt you are the Son of God!" (14:33).

The faith of the Christian community has shaped this beautiful Gospel story. The plight of the disciples in the boat reflects the church's own tensions and fears as it faces the chaos of a sometimes hostile world. The church believes that its Lord has given it a share in his own power over sin and darkness. But fear and doubt are realities too, and they seem to smother faith's vitality. But even then prayer is not in vain. Even we "in the boat," we "of little faith," can be lifted from the waves by a merciful Lord.

But if resurrection faith has helped shape this story, there is little doubt that it is rooted in the community's memory of the touching bond between Jesus of Nazareth and his disciples. The early Christians too were called by Jesus and were given a share in his mission. Their response too was flawed by fear and hesitation. But with the church, as with the disciples, Jesus' reaction is one of unending love. The community's experience of resurrection as reconciliation could not have been unrelated with what they knew of Jesus before his death. Their joy was ecstatic; they discovered in the liberating love of the Risen Lord the same fellowship that had bound Jesus to his improbable followers. He had chosen them, men practically identical with the "sick" he came to save. He endured their dullness. He dealt with them honestly, exactingly; but neither his critique nor his commands were ever destructive. The disciples' record was not good: They complained, they misunderstood, they quarreled, they deserted, they denied. Only one was lost. But the part of the story that becomes "Gospel"—"good news"—is that in the face of the Master they failed, the disciples detected the infinite compassion of God, and they committed this memory to the church.

Jesus and the Outcasts

The Gospel portrayal of the disciples helps us learn about Jesus who not only endured them but loved them. There are other groups Jesus was drawn to, and we can gain insight from them too. One of the most intriguing Gospel themes is Jesus' love for the poor and the outcasts. Here again the ministry of the Kingdom is the key to the Gospels' emphasis.

Like many theological currents of the Old Testament, the Kingdom of God theme matured into a complex notion, and its precise contours are often difficult to define. But one important aspect of the Kingdom tradition, from a Gospel point of view, is that the prime beneficiaries of the future Kingdom would be the "poor." This facet of the Kingdom theology can be traced to the Near Eastern experience of monarchy. The sovereign, in most legal codes of the ancient cultures of the Middle East, was responsible for defending the rights of the poor and the weak. The emergence of the monarchy in Israel, where the king was in principle the vicar for Yahweh King, absorbed this aspect of monarchical justice. The repeated failure of the Jewish kings to protect the defenseless in Israel took on the added burden of failing to accomplish Yahweh's own responsibility to the poor. The vigor of the prophets' critique of social injustice finds much of its explanation in this understanding. It became clear that when Yahweh himself would establish his rule over Israel and the nations—when the network of relationships between men and nations was as Yahweh would have it—the Kingdom would indeed be "good news for the poor." The "poor"—which includes the widows, the orphans, and the outcasts who are unable to defend themselves—will have Yahweh King as their protector because Yahweh alone is all merciful. Thus the privileges of the poor in the future Kingdom do not derive from their pitiful situation nor from any supposed spiritual disposition that one might attribute to the poor. The poor receive particular attention in the Kingdom because of Yahweh. God's mercy and compassion for the defenseless assures benefits to the poor in the Kingdom. The poor are singled out not because poverty is a requirement for piety but because God is merciful.

This aspect of the Kingdom theme must be kept in mind if we want to understand the ministry of Jesus and his association with the poor and the outcasts. His program of preaching "good news to the poor" (cf. Luke 4:18; 7:22) was not a sentimental gesture but a deliberate role fraught with consequences. The poor were the special object of Jesus' ministry because he was announcing the Kingdom of God. The most urgent responsibility of the messenger of the Kingdom was to reveal in work and word the compassion and mercy of the King.

The Gospels underline Jesus' accomplishment of this Kingdom ministry not only by cataloguing his actions but by recording his associations. Jesus eats with the poor and sinners. He is a friend of tax gatherers and prostitutes and other unsound members of first-century Jewish society. The Gospel evidence is exceptionally rich here. Jesus invites sinners to his home and shares a meal with them (Luke 15:1-2). He enjoys table fellowship with the very people whom Jewish law bans as "unclean" (cf. Mark 2:15). This emphasis on table fellowship is notable in a Semitic culture where sharing a meal was considered more of a sharing of life than simply a casual association.

The Gospels' reporting of the consistently hostile reaction of the Jewish leaders to Jesus' association with the poor emphasizes the singularity of his behavior. They resent Jesus' friendship with segments of society whose status placed them in the circle of the officially unclean. The "murmuring" of the official religious leadership becomes a threatening chorus as Jesus' ministry progresses. Scribes and Pharisees complain to Jesus' disciples because their master eats with tax collectors and sinners (Mark 2:16). His Pharisee host resents his association with

70

a sinful woman (Luke 7:39). They mock the welcome he gives to sinners (Luke 15:1-2) and take offense at his attention to Zacchaeus (Luke 19:7).

Many of Jesus' parables and sayings appear to be a direct challenge to this growing hostility. It is not the "healthy" the physician should seek out but the "sick," not the self-righteous but sinners (Mark 2:17). Jesus pointedly tells his Pharisee host not to invite his wealthy friends to his feasts, but beggars, cripples, the lame, and the blind (Luke 14:12-13). The heavenly banquet hall will be filled not with the rich but with the poor (Luke 14:21). The ultimate judgment of human worth will be decided on the basis of their attention to those in need (Matthew 25:31-46).

Those who consider themselves well-off are targets of uncomplimentary comparisons with the poor: Lazarus is saved, but the rich man perishes (Luke 16:19-31); the tax collector's prayer is heard, but the Pharisee's is not (Luke 18:9-14); the poor widow's single coin is far more acceptable than the offerings of the rich (Luke 21:1-4). These jolting contrasts between poor and rich, between those who are objects of concern and forgiveness by Yahweh and those who blindly consider themselves dispensed from a need for radical help, find their most quotable expression in the Beatitudes. The version of Luke, the evangelist who gives the most attention to Jesus' dealings with the poor, maintains a blunt tone.

Blest are you poor; the reign of God is yours.
Blest are you who hunger; you shall be filled.
Blest are you who are weeping; you shall laugh . . .
But woe to you rich, for your consolation is now.
Woe to you who are full; you shall go hungry.
Woe to you who laugh now; you shall weep in your grief
(Luke 6:20-21, 24-25).

The Gospels, then, speak often and eloquently of Jesus' association with the poor and outcasts. As was the case with the Gospel portrayal of the disciples, this emphasis has the immediate purpose of guiding the church's own ministry. The Christian community was to be as sensitive to the needs of the poor and as careful to avoid the seduction of wealth as Jesus was. But the strength of this Gospel appeal finds its source in Jesus; he was this way. He had the integrity and the compassion to move freely with those whom his society had shunted aside.

This Gospel image becomes even more compelling when we recall the social conditions of Jesus' day. The poor were plentiful, and they were desperate: crushed by a system of taxation, oppressed politically, socially, religiously. We can only imagine the liberating effect that Jesus, a man who spoke with authority and grace, had when he moved with the poor and proclaimed that the Kingdom of God was theirs.

But Jesus' ministry to the poor was not calculated demagoguery. The poor were not pawns in a religious power play, although Jesus' enemies may have feared that such was his motive. When you sift the Gospel evidence, there is no case for picturing Jesus as a doctrinaire radical. He loved the poor, but he did not idealize them. The parable of the wedding feast comes to mind (cf. Matthew 22:1-14). The Kingdom of God is depicted in traditional imagery as a great banquet. The guests originally invited, landowners and businessmen (Matthew 22:5; cf. Luke who emphasizes as often the contrast between rich and poor, 14:16-24), make excuses, and they fail to honor the invitation. The Lord of the banquet then throws open the feast to all, bad and good. When the guests are assembled, the King enters the hall to greet those who share in the meal. But he comes on one guest who has not put on a wedding garment, a sign of repentance and of new life. His poverty is no excuse for his lack of response to the Kingdom, and he is put outside. Jesus' point is clear: Social position, high or low, is no guarantee of salvation; only a genuine response to the Gospel is.

That Jesus' love for the poor was not calculated or opportunistic is indicated by the fact that he moved as freely with the non-poor. His disciples were from the lower classes but not below the poverty line. Galilean fishermen were a propertied class. Jesus and his father seemed to have been village craftsmen (Mark 6:3). The Gospels testify to a number of instances where Jesus circulated with middle- and upper-class people. He dines with Pharisees (cf. Luke 7:36f.; 11:37ff.; 14:1ff.). He befriends Zacchaeus, "the chief tax collector and a wealthy man" (Luke 19:2) and deliberately chooses to stay at his house. He deals with the Roman centurion as an equal (Luke 7:1ff.). Rich and powerful characters star in many of Jesus' parables. There is the wealthy landowner (Matthew 13:24-30), the pearl merchant (Matthew 13:45-46), the king and his officials (Matthew 18:21ff.), the owner of an estate who hires laborers all day long (Matthew 20:1ff.), the absentee landlord who owns a vineyard (Matthew 21:33ff.), the master of the household who dispenses enormous sums for investment (Matthew 25:14ff.), the owner of a hundred sheep (Luke 15:1ff.), the crafty head steward (Luke 16:1ff.), the unjust judge (Luke 18:1-8). In many of these stories, of course, the rich and the powerful are criticized severely, but not always. The rich and the ways of the rich are sometimes just a part of the scenery of everyday life. Jesus utilizes them for his illustration, and he feels comfortable with them. He knew the rich and the powerful. He even seems bemused at their sensitivity for status and recognition (cf. Luke 14:7-11). But he was not owned by them.

Nor was Jesus in the pocket of the poor. His excoriation of the rich and his driving compassion for the poor do not mean that a different Gospel was fitted to each. The call to newness of life, to repentance, to indiscriminate love was directed to all, rich and poor. Jesus' integrity finds a grim witness in his death: Neither rich nor poor would stand beside him.

Jesus and Women

An attempt to discover something about Jesus from those who were close to him in the Gospels has led to the disciples and to the outcasts. We turn now to a final group whose identity merges both of these categories: the women. They had fellowship with the outcasts because of their standing in Palestinian society. They are to be numbered with the disciples because the Gospels unanimously insist that the most faithful followers Jesus had were women.

Our contemporary society, at least in a good deal of the Western world, seems to be awakening gradually to the dignity of women and their right to full participation in every function of society. All of the subtle ways that bind women to unequal status become increasingly embarrassing and intolerable: an exploitive sexism, discriminatory compensation for employment, a diffuse image of woman as man's playmate. Almost every legitimate liberation movement—as the struggle for women's rights is—generates a renewed appreciation of one's heritage. The energy of the Black movement has discovered scores of Black men and women who played key roles in America's past but whose contributions had been neglected or overlooked. The Gospels offer the same liberating discovery if we simply read them and note carefully the part women play there.

To fully appreciate the impact of the Gospel material, we should be aware of the situation of women in Palestinian Judaism at the time of Jesus. Although our sources of information are few, they are sufficient to give us at least a general idea.

The role of women in Jewish society was restricted to domestic circles. The first-century Jewish philosopher Philo offers this suggestion regarding a woman's proper domain: "The women are best suited to the indoor life which never strays from the house, within which the middle door is taken by the maidens as their boundary, and the outer door by those who have reached full womanhood." In another place, he adds: "A woman, then, should not be a busybody, meddling with matters outside her household concerns, but should seek a life of seclusion. She should not show herself off like a vagrant in the streets before the eyes of other men, except when she has to go to the temple." Josephus, also writing in the first century, offers a similarly demeaning picture: "The woman, says the Law, is in all things inferior to the man. Let her accordingly be submissive, not for her humiliation, but that she may be directed; for the authority has been given by God to the man."

Joachim Jeremias, an expert on first-century Judaism, notes that this "inferiority" extended also to religious matters. A woman was not permitted full access to the Temple; she was restricted to an outer courtyard. The religious obligations expected of her were the same as a slave's. She did not have to recite the Shema prayer that every male Jew was expected to pray each morning and evening. The reason given was that a woman, like a slave, was not the mistress of her own time.

Most of the restrictive legislation dealing with the public appearances of women were moral in intent. The woman was viewed as an object of lust, and morality was to be safeguarded by keeping her out of the public eye. Even when a woman had to appear on the streets, she was to veil her face. A famous injunction of the rabbis was: "Do not speak much with a woman on the street." This saying applied even to one's own wife, who was expected to maintain a discreet distance behind her husband if the two had to venture out together.

Although the picture is not complete, one easily senses the minimal role women were afforded in Jesus' day. In fact, women were more restricted in first-century Judaism than in previous periods of Israel's history. Jesus' own dealings with women are a bracing contrast to this picture.

Christian piety has always appreciated the significant attention given in the Gospels to Mary, the mother of Jesus. The birth narratives, particularly that of Luke, portray Mary as a faithful Israelite, a woman whose destiny as the mother of the Messiah is signed by the Spirit of God. All of the evangelists position Mary at the crucifixion scene—in stark contrast to the disciples' absence. Both John and Luke connect Mary with the life of the first community—John by noting Jesus' words assigning Mary to the care of the "beloved disciple" (John 19:27), and Luke by indicating her presence with the Apostles in Jerusalem after the resurrection (Acts 1:14). Gospel texts such as these are the foundation of the Catholic church's continued reverence for the woman who shared her life with Jesus. This strong tradition has been called upon in recent church statements that attempt to define the role of women in the church. But equally revealing, if perhaps somewhat neglected, are the more ordinary contacts Jesus had with women in the course of his ministry.

Jesus obviously did not feel compelled to follow the rabbinic strictures demanding public avoidance of women. The evidence cuts across all four Gospels. Many of those whom Jesus heals are women. In fact, the very first healing narrative in the synoptic Gospel accounts is Simon's mother-in-law whom Jesus cures of a fever (cf. Mark 1:29-31). Jesus cures the woman with a hemorrhage (Matthew 9:20), the daughter of Jairus (Luke 8:54), the daughter of the Syro-Phoenician woman (Matthew 15:21-28), and the woman with a crippling disease (Luke 13:10-17). When the Pharisees protest this last cure, because it is done on the Sabbath, Jesus insists that this "daughter of Abraham" is more precious than the Sabbath legislation. Luke also relates the cure of the widow of Naim's son, because he took pity on her (Luke 7:11-17).

Jesus freely associates with women in the course of his ministry. All three synoptics record that Jesus was anointed with oil by a "sinful woman." Luke (7:36-50) places this anointing in the context of a meal with the Pharisees and has Jesus defend at length the woman's sincerity. Both Luke and John record Jesus' special friendship with the sisters Mary and Martha (cf. Luke 10:38; John 11:5). John also narrates the beautiful story of Jesus and the Samaritan woman in chapter 4. Their chance meeting at the well initiates an almost playful conversation between the Jewish rabbi and the woman whose colorful past Jesus is well aware of. The liberty of talking with a woman alone, and a Samaritan at that, shocks the disciples into embarrassed silence (John 4:27). The fourth Gospel also gives us the incident of Jesus and the woman caught in adultery (John 8:1-11). The story is missing in several important early manuscripts, hence it may not have been part of the original edition of the Gospel. But its style and tone place it squarely in the Johannine tradition.

Perhaps the most revealing evidence of all is the unique position women have among Jesus' followers. They are not counted among the Twelve, nor are they formally addressed as "disciples" in the Gospels. But their fidelity makes a staggering contrast to their male counterparts. At several points in the Gospels, the evangelists, particularly but not exclusively Luke, make explicit reference to the women who followed Jesus in his ministry. At the beginning of chapter 8, Luke provides this illuminating summary of Jesus' ministry:

After this he journeyed through towns and villages preaching and proclaiming the good news of the kingdom of God. The Twelve accompanied him, and also some women who had been cured of evil spirits and maladies; Mary called the Magdalene, from whom seven devils had gone out, Joanna, the wife of Herod's steward Chuza, Susanna, and many others who were assisting them out of their means (8:1-3).

This remarkable text not only associates the women with the Twelve but states that the women had been supporting the entire mission. The most telling evidence is in the Passion story; here again, the support cuts across all four Gospel accounts. As we have seen, the Passion tradition either explicitly states or, in the case of Luke and John, embarrassingly intimates that the disciples of Jesus deserted him and fled at the moment of the arrest. The betrayal by Judas and the denial of Peter climax this grim account of discipleship failure. But perhaps one should qualify this by noting that the failure is restricted to the men. Putting it this way is not an attempt to be clever; it is an acknowledgment of one of the most insistent features of the Passion tradition: the women did not desert Jesus.

Luke seems to signal this fidelity during the procession of events from the praetorium to Golgotha. "A great crowd of people followed him, including women who beat their breasts and lamented over him. Jesus turned to them and said: 'Daughters of Jerusalem, do not weep for me. Weep for yourselves and for your children' " (23:27-28). All four accounts refer to the presence of women near the cross as Jesus dies. (Matthew 27:55; Mark 15:40; Luke 23:49; John 19:25). Their presence is not attributable to curiosity or defeat. In the synoptic presentation, they are associated with the Roman centurion who witnesses Jesus' death and confesses his identity as the Son of God. In each case, the women are identified as those who "had followed Jesus" from Galilee to Jerusalem and "ministered to his needs." In the Gospel tradition, being present to Jesus and following him in his ministry from Galilee to Jerusalem defines discipleship.

This testimony to the women's faithful discipleship is carried over into the resurrection story. Again, a major consensus unites the various Gospel presentations. All four Gospels state that women were the first to discover the empty tomb. In Matthew and John, women are the first to whom the Risen Lord appears. And in all of the accounts, the women are given the responsibility of bringing the Easter news to the other disciples.

The origin and development of the complex resurrection narratives are topics we cannot do justice to here. But the crucial role played by women in all layers of the narrative tradition cannot be ignored. At the very least, the tradition suggests that women were major participants in the life of the primitive community. There is even reason to surmise that the Gospel tradition preserved the evidence of this role somewhat reluctantly. Luke, for example, admits that the Apostles were sceptical about the women's report of an empty tomb: "The story seemed like nonsense and they refused to believe them" (24:11). By the time the Gospels were finally written down, much of the early community's liberalism regarding women had already eroded. The pastoral epistles, written toward the end of the first century, give women a role in the church not unlike that of women in the synagogue in rabbinic Judaism. The author of the First Epistle to Timothy, for example, urges women to be quiet and submissive and seems to limit sharply their role in the community (cf. I Timothy 2:11-15). But passages like this should be read in their proper context. One of the problems the pastoral epistles attempted to combat was heretical groups developing in the early church. Many of these splinter communities happened to be egalitarian in nature. Thus the author's injunctions about the place of women in the church should not be taken as an absolute norm but must be understood as part of a reaction to a crisis.

The extraordinary place that women maintain in the Gospel tradition survived, then, against the grain. There is little doubt that the tenacity of the Gospels' tribute to the women disciples was due to the fact that Jesus' own radical departure from the mores of his day could not be denied.

Jesus' attitude toward women and toward their role in the Kingdom displays the same freedom and integrity that he showed to the poor and to the rich. Status or inheritance did not circumscribe the beauty of the person nor his or her ability to respond to the Gospel. The few words of Jesus that deal directly with women reflect this same integrity. A lustful heart is no better than adultery; both spring from a twisted view of sexuality and human relationships (Matthew 5:27-28). Jesus pointedly refuses to become embroiled in rabbinic discussions about the grounds for divorce. Matthew, more sensitive to the Jewish context of the Gospel material, has restored the Markan incident to its original setting. Some Pharisees set out to ensnare Jesus by debating with him a current question: "Can a man divorce his wife for any reason whatever?" (Matthew 19:3). The two great rabbinic schools of Hillel and Shammai were divided on this question. Divorce was permitted under Mosaic Law (cf. Deuteronomy 24:1-4), but interpretation of the sufficient grounds was controverted. The strict school of Shammai believed that only adultery justified divorce; the Hillel school allowed divorce for numerous reasons, some as trifling as the wife's inability to cook or her lack of physical beauty. Jesus' reply does not choose sides. Instead, he appeals to a more fundamental view of marriage reflected in the traditions of Genesis: "Have you not read that at the beginning the Creator made them male and female and declared, 'For this reason a man shall leave his father and mother and cling to his wife, and the two shall become as one?' " (Matthew 19:5). Jesus' citation is not only an injunction against divorce; even more basically, it reveals an attitude toward the human person and the mystery of sexuality that is one of the supreme expressions of the Old Testament. The will of God expressed in creation is a call to unity, a unity in which male and female have an integral part. It is here that the image of God himself is found.

As is always the case in the Gospels, Jesus' teaching is a reflection of what he himself is and does. Jesus' respect for women and his freedom to associate with them—a freedom remarkable in his time—mesh perfectly with his teaching on what a person is. Paul, a man not entirely free from a rabbinic view of the place of women, nevertheless reflects the teaching of Jesus in a capital passage from his letter to the Galatian Christians:

Each of you is a son of God because of your faith in Christ Jesus. All of you who have been baptized into Christ have clothed yourselves with him. There does not exist among you Jew or Greek, slave or freeman, male or female. All are one in Christ Jesus (3:26-28).

The Gospel account of Jesus' most privileged relationships do tell us something about the man. Perhaps the picture is not as satisfying as we might like. The very nature of the Gospel material should make us hesitant to think we could learn *too* much. It is difficult, if not impossible, to learn the precise way that Jesus dealt with his own. We do not have neat accounts of the delicacy of his approach, of his finesse, or his repartee. The extended conversations we do have, such as John's account of the Samaritan woman or Jesus' last discourse with the disciples, owe tribute to the tradition that maintained them as well as to the characters who originated them. Thus we can make conclusions about Jesus' "psychology" only with a large amount of educated guesses.

But what we do learn about Jesus' relationships in the Gospel, and therefore about Jesus himself, is the element of the unexpected. It is unexpected that Jesus' disciples should be so fallible. It is unexpected that he should be most comfortable with the poor and the outcasts. It is unexpected that he should associate so freely and so often with women. "Unexpected" because neither the concerns of the early church nor the conditions of Jesus' own time prepare us for these associations. It is this bracing quality of the unexpected that characterizes so much of what we are able to learn about Jesus from the Gospels.

The Gospel portrait of Jesus begins to take shape: a man sensitive to the traditions of his people but at the same time supremely free, a man with such magnetism that his very presence was an authority, a man whose friends were not abandoned, even when they were disappointing.

Jesus' courage and conviction earned him opposition and hostility. But a man's enemies may be as revealing as his friends. Many of the charges against Jesus, as recorded in the Gospels, are based on the fact that his disciples were unkempt, that he associated with the lawless, that he befriended women, and that he spoke and acted as if he were on a mission from God. Such a portrait could have originated only with Jesus of Nazareth. That it is precisely this portrait that the Gospel tradition maintained could only be the work of the Spirit.

Chapter 4

Jesus
Speaks

If friends and enemies reveal who we are, so do our words. The task of searching out the Gospel portrait of Jesus must include a careful listening to what Jesus says.

As with every aspect of the Gospel story, the very nature of the sources we have available imposes certain limits on our analysis. The evangelists do not provide random samples of Jesus' everyday conversations. The Gospel tradition preserved the words of Jesus that touched the life of the church: not casual conversations but the penetrating wisdom of the master teacher. And even the words we do have are not transcripts from a tape. What Jesus said has been lovingly handled and shaped by the very life of the church that listens to and applies his wisdom. Even in the case of crucial sayings, such as the words of institution at the Last Supper or the Lord's Prayer, there is no perfect harmony among the various accounts. But the alterations that took place in the long process leading up to the Gospels do not suppress the voice of Jesus. If we listen carefully, we can hear the freshness and authority of the teacher of Nazareth.

The Kingdom Is Coming

To appreciate the significance of Jesus' associations as recorded in the Gospels, we had to appeal to his ministry of the Kingdom. The same key unlocks the meaning of many of his words. Not all of the sayings of Jesus found in the Gospels can be filed neatly under the Kingdom theme, but Jesus' convictions about the Kingdom and the Kingdom's God touch almost everything he said and did.

We have stated that the energy and conviction of Jesus' preaching are rooted in his belief that the Kingdom of God was near at hand. John the Baptist had preached a similar message: "Reform your lives! The reign of God is at hand" (Matthew 3:2). With Jesus, this urgency quickened. John never claimed to be the one whose advent triggered the coming of the Kingdom, but Jesus seemed vividly aware that his own ministry was the start of a new age. He was a prophet, but something more than a prophet.

When we sift through Jesus' statements about the coming of the Kingdom, there seems to be a certain ambivalence. Many parables insist that the Kingdom comes slowly, almost imperceptibly. The Kingdom of God is like a mustard seed, the smallest of all seeds. But an insignificant beginning eventually blooms into a large tree (Matthew 13:31-32). Or the Kingdom is like a bit of leaven folded into dough. It gradually transforms the loaf (Matthew 13:33). Or the Kingdom is like a handful of seed that a man scatters on the ground. While he sleeps, the seed begins the struggle towards the harvest. Jesus prays, "your Kingdom come" (Matthew 6:10), a prayer for the future.

Thus some of the parables and sayings of Jesus refer to the Kingdom as a future event whose full impact must be preceded by slow and patient growth. But these sayings must be balanced with an equally urgent insistence that the Kingdom is somehow present now, in the very words and works of the Kingdom's herald. In the Gospel of Luke, some Pharisees put a direct question to Jesus about the Kingdom's timetable. "He replied: 'You cannot tell by careful watching when the reign of God will come. Neither is it a matter of reporting that it is "here" or "there." The reign of God is already in your midst'"

(17:20-21). In another incident, some Pharisees interpret Jesus' miracles as evidence that he is in league with Satan. There comes this quick response: "But if it is by the Spirit of God that I expel demons, then the reign of God has overtaken you" (Matthew 12:28).

This confused timetable for the Kingdom, seemingly both present and future, has baffled biblical scholars. No neat solution is likely to be found. Jesus seems to say both. The fullness of the Kingdom, the complete expression of God's kingly rule over Israel and the nations, awaits the future. But that does not mean we are stranded in the Kingdom's waiting room, victims of an uncertain future. Now is the time of decision. Now is the time when we either open our lives to a new age of grace or wall ourselves up in a life of egoism. This urgency pulsates throughout most of the preaching of Jesus. The Kingdom may be future, but the choice is now.

We can catch some of the restless drive of Jesus' mission in the way he calls his disciples. He strides into their lives and summons them: Come—now. Many of his sayings and parables have the same urgency. The Kingdom of God is like a buried treasure, don't you see? The one who finds it sells everything to buy that field (Matthew 13:44). The Kingdom of God is like a merchant who searches for fine pearls. When he finds one great pearl, he sells everything to buy that pearl (Matthew 13:45f.). These insistent parables seem to grip the listener by the lapels, to press the urgency of the critical now.

But Jesus' preaching was not limited to an excited announcement of a time of opportunity. The approach of the Kingdom demands a precise response, and the sayings of Jesus define it. Those who perceive the Kingdom's nearness are to repent. The Greek word that expresses this repentance in several sayings of Jesus is metanoia—literally, a "change of mind." The impact of the word implies a complete reform, a radical change in priorities in view of God's reaching out to his world. "I assure you, unless you turn around, and become like little children, you will not enter the Kingdom" (Matthew 18:3). The call is for a complete reassessment of the priorities that rule our lives. Many of the "renouncement" sayings of Jesus are simply alternate ways of stressing the need for radical conversion and full commitment to the Kingdom. "If a man wishes to come after me, he must deny his very self, take up his cross, and follow in my steps" (Mark 8:34). "Whoever would preserve his life will lose it, but whoever loses his life for my sake and the Gospel's will preserve it" (Mark 8:35). Response to the Kingdom absolutely must be the first priority; no human tie or obligation can be counted before it. "If anyone comes to me without turning his back on his father and mother, his wife and his children, his brothers and sisters, indeed his very self, he cannot be my follower" (Luke 14:26). "Moreover, everyone who has given up home, brothers and sisters, father or mother, wife or children or property for my sake will receive many times as much and inherit everlasting life" (Matthew 19:29).

Those who hear the Kingdom's call should be aware of the cost. "If one of you decides to build a tower, will he not first sit down and calculate the outlay to see if he has enough money to complete the project?" "Or if a king is about to march on another king to do battle with him, will he not sit down first and consider whether, with ten thousand men, he can withstand an enemy coming against him with twenty thousand?" (Luke 14:28, 31). Any unconsidered attempt to follow Jesus' ministry of the Kingdom is brought up short: " 'I will be your follower, Lord, but first let me take leave of my people at home.' Jesus answered him, 'Whoever puts his hand to the plow but keeps looking back is unfit for the reign of God' " (Luke 9:61f.).

Jesus' "scandal" sayings are similar. The Greek word *scandalon* is quite different from what our moral use of the term implies. "Scandal" in the New Testament does not refer primarily to some sin that has an attractive horror about it. *Scandalon* means "obstacle," something that stands in the way. Jesus' sayings about "scandal" refer to the unyielding priority of the Kingdom. "If your hand or your foot is a 'scandal,' cut it off and throw it from you! Better to enter life maimed or crippled . . ." "If your eye is a scandal, gouge it out and cast it from you! Better to enter life with one eye . . ." (Matthew 18:8ff).

The call to the Kingdom seems to hound Jesus' listeners. No excuse, however reasonable, is admitted. No tie, however intimate or compelling, can be preferred. The invited guests in Luke's parable of the Kingdom banquet recite them all: "I have bought some land and must go out and inspect it. Please excuse me." "I have bought five yoke of oxen and I am going out to test them. Please excuse me." "I am newly married and so I cannot come." But to respond less than fully to the Kingdom is to forfeit the choice of life itself: "I tell you not one of those invited shall taste a morsel of my dinner" (Luke 14:24).

An incredible proportion of the Gospel sayings of Jesus have this taut, demanding tone. The sampling we have given is by no means exhaustive. What is behind it all? What is the basis of this urgent announcement of the Kingdom? What does "putting the Kingdom first" really mean? If one is to "repent," to "reform," to radically change one's priorities, then to what? What is to be the priority of the Kingdom, and what is the basis for Jesus' saying so? When we search through the sayings of Jesus with these kinds of questions, we are coming close to the center of the Gospel portrait.

The God of the Kingdom

If a reader of the Gospel wishes to perceive the reason for Jesus' urgent announcement of the coming of the Kingdom, and the teaching that derives from it, then she or he must sense something of Jesus' experience of God. For Jesus' proclamation of the Kingdom was not a "program" or a campaign. He was not selling anything, nor was he wrapped up in some sort of "cause." His tireless ministry cannot be reduced to a plan of social reform. Jesus was a Jew, a thoroughly religious man. The vital impulse that animated his life of service was not a neat deduction of reason nor a vague conviction that this was the way things had to be done. Jesus' way of life was a response to his God. It was obedience.

To probe anyone's experience of God, let alone that of Jesus, is a daring, ambitious task. Much of that experience remains ineffable, untouchable. We can only hope to grasp at the edge of the mystery. Our image of God is as intimate as our image of ourselves. Trying to appreciate Jesus' experience of God is complicated by our own faith in him. Mature Christian belief proclaims that Jesus is human and divine, man and "more than" man. This "more than"—which Christian faith has always confessed tenaciously but can never comprehend fully—can have a side effect of robbing Jesus of his humanity. If Jesus is divine, as the believer affirms, then we confer on Jesus the attributes of divinity. He must be all-knowing, eternal, somehow exempt from the ignorance and anxiety that make up the ordinary human experience. If Jesus is divine, how can we conceive of him as "learning" about God or having an "experience" of God?

But genuine Christian theology has always reacted against a perception of Christ that attempts to protect his divinity at the expense of his humanity. Both ends of the mystery must be maintained to do justice to belief. Jesus was a man, a Jew, a citizen of the first century. Nothing of the mystery of his divinity can be allowed to falsify the human dimensions of his life. He shared every aspect of human experience except that of alienation from God, an aspect that is not genuinely human in the first place. And his "sharing" should not be conceived as play acting. Jesus did not go through the motions of being human. He *was* human. He had to learn, to search, to be a fellow traveler in the sometimes tortuous pilgrimage of human existence.

Jesus, then, would have learned of God in the same way that most of his countrymen did. The rich religious heritage of Judaism was shared with Jesus by his family, his friends, his teachers, and the institutions of Jewish life. The Gospels do not provide us with details about Jesus' early religious education, but we can assume this part of his experience. Besides the instruction and example of family and home, the focus of religious education at the time of Jesus was the synagogue. Luke informs us that Jesus began his public ministry when he entered the synagogue of Nazareth "on the sabbath as he was in the habit of doing" (Luke 4:16). Numerous other references in the Gospel place Jesus as a visiting rabbi in the local synagogues.

The synagogue should not be confused with the Temple. There was only one temple in Judaism, the Jerusalem Temple that had been the center of Jewish religious life since the time of Solomon. There the ritual of sacrifice was carried out with exacting care. There too, in the sacred inner sanctuary of the Holy of Holies, was to be found the sure presence of Yahweh among his people. Jerusalem's Temple was therefore the center of worship and pilgrimage for all Jews.

But the backbone of Jewish life since the Babylonian exile in the sixth century was the synagogue. The Temple, after all, was inaccessible for most Jews, especially those outside Palestine. But each Jewish settlement would have at least one synagogue. If the focus of the Temple was ritual sacrifice, the focus of the synagogue was the Scriptures, the sacred Torah of Israel. The priests were the guardians of the Temple worship; but the rabbi, the master of the Law, was the dominant figure of synagogue life. On the Sabbath, the Jews would assemble in their local synagogue to hear readings from Scripture, to be instructed on their meaning, and to pray in common. The readings were on a cyclic basis. The text was read in Hebrew; but, at the time of Jesus, most of the people probably could understand only Aramaic, so that the original version was followed by a translation or paraphrase in Aramaic. A rabbi then would give a homily to explain the meaning of the text. If a visiting rabbi was attending the service, he could be invited to say a few words.

The function of the synagogue was not limited to the prescribed Sabbath observance. It became the natural focus of the social and political life of the local community. When the Temple was destroyed in the holocaust of 70 A.D., the strength of the synagogue would play a major role in the survival of Jewish religious life.

Not all of customary Jewish religious life was confined to formal observances at the Temple or synagogue. The faithful Jew was expected to cultivate a life of personal prayer in the privacy of his home. At dawn and again at nightfall, the Jew was to recite Israel's creed, the famous *Shema* prayer found in the book of Deuteronomy (6:4-5):

Hear, O Israel! The Lord is our God, the Lord alone! Therefore, you shall love the Lord, our God, with all your heart, with all your soul, and with all your strength.

The twice-daily recitation of the *Shema* was considered an absolute minimum of observance. Along with it, the truly faithful Jew would set aside three periods each day to pray the *Tephilla* or prayers of benediction. In the morning and evening, the *Tephilla* would be joined to the recitation of the prescribed *Shema*. At three in the afternoon, the prayers of praise and benediction again would be said, coinciding with the time when the afternoon sacrifice was being offered in the Temple.

In all of these cases, it was understood that private, personal prayer was to be joined to the formal prayers. Therefore, Jesus, like his fellow believers, grew up in a religious tradition that had prayer woven into the fabric of daily life.

The core of Jewish religious life, then, was reflection on the Scripture and prayer. There is Gospel evidence that both of these forces had a deep influence on Jesus' own religious experience. A profound reverence for the Scriptures was the starting point of all Jewish piety. The sacred Torah was the revelation of the God of Israel. It spoke of God's love for his people, of his expectations, of his promise. To be faithful meant simply to be obedient to the Torah. There are several references in the Gospels to Jesus' obedience to or "fulfillment" of the Scriptures. Behind these references stands the simple fact that Jesus, as a faithful Jew, must have found the direction of his own life and ministry in a prayerful reading of Scripture. Such is the implication of the powerful temptation scenes found in the Gospels of Matthew and Luke. Satan tries to dissuade the young Messiah from his chosen course by offers of power, of adulation, and of misplaced trust. Each of Jesus' replies is a quotation of Scripture: "Scripture has it, 'Not on bread alone shall man live' " (Matthew 4:4; Deuteronomy 8:3). "Scripture also says, 'You shall not put the Lord your God to the test' " (Matthew 4:7 =Deuteronomy 6:16). "Scripture has it, 'You shall do homage to the Lord your God; him alone shall you adore' " (Matthew 4:8 =Deuteronomy 6:13).

These Gospel scenes are highly dramatized. The temptations they envision reflect not only Jesus' experience as he began his ministry but the types of challenges he repeatedly met in the course of his service. The Pharisees' constant demand for some clinching "sign" of his credentials, Peter and the disciples' attempts to dissuade him from his brand of messiahship (Mark 8:33), all are labeled as "temptations" by Jesus.

At other crucial points in this ministry, the Gospels note Jesus' appeal to Scripture. He turns back a challenge to his healing ministry by telling his opponents to read the text of Hosea, "It is mercy I desire and not sacrifice" (Matthew 9:13). His furious reaction to the improprieties of the

Temple trade is accompanied by his quotation of Isaiah, "My house shall be called a house of prayer" (Matthew 21:13). His foreboding prediction of the disciples' desertion is understood against the prophetic text of Zachariah, "I will strike the shepherd and the sheep of the flock will be dispersed" (Mark 14:27). Each of the synoptic Gospels places the verse of a psalm (albeit a different one) on the lips of Jesus as he dies.

We must be careful not to take these various examples too literally. In most cases, they are not meant to be reports of Scripture quotations that Jesus may have cited on a particular occasion; rather, they represent the church's own efforts to understand the life of Jesus in the light of the Old Testament Scriptures. But there can be no doubt that at the root of these traditions lies the justifying fact that Jesus himself drew the source and direction of his ministry from a penetrating reflection on God's word.

Jesus' appeal to the Scriptures should not be thought of as a rummaging through Israel's sacred book for particular texts that could be applied literally to the circumstances at hand. Such a literalism would have been foreign to him, as it was to the early Christian writers who used biblical texts with great freedom. What Jesus sought in the Scriptures was the voice of his God, the God whose will was Jesus' "meat" (John 4:34). Jesus' obedience to the Scriptures was the expression of an intimate relationship to his Father, a relationship that bursts into expression in the prayer of Jesus. The Gospels, particularly that of Luke, refer to Jesus at prayer. Jesus' urgent ministry of preaching and healing is punctuated by moments of prayer in solitude (cf. Luke 5:16; 6:12, etc.). Luke implies too that the olive grove of Gethsemane was a customary refuge of prayer (Luke 22:39). Jesus' prayer at the crisis of his suffering and death is instinctive. It must have been in these moments of prayer that the religious experience of Jesus was forged. And here too we find the source of his ministry of the Kingdom.

Only infrequently do the Gospels attempt to describe the contents of Jesus' prayer, but the texts we do have are revealing. Each of the Gospels begins Jesus' ministry with a profound religious experience. In the synoptic Gospels, this takes place at Jesus' baptism by John. In the fourth Gospel, the baptism of Jesus is not mentioned explicitly, but the testimony of John about Jesus' receiving the experience seems to refer to the same tradition that the earlier Gospels record. The function of the baptism scene is to serve as a formal commissioning of Jesus as he launches his ministry of the Kingdom. It testifies that Jesus had received the fullness of the Spirit of God. He is God's Son, his faithful servant. The reader is left with no doubts about the identity of the one who is about to perform the works of God.

But even if the scene has been formalized in the Gospel tradition, there is no reason to deny that at the root of the tradition was a profound religious experience of Jesus himself. Perhaps the preaching of John, or Jesus' own experience in prayer and reflection on the Scriptures, had led him to the realization of his call to announce the Kingdom. One of the most revealing aspects of the baptism scene, for our purposes, is the insistence on Jesus' sonship. The "voice from the heavens," a Jewish reverential way of referring to Yahweh himself, declared, "This is my beloved Son. My favor rests on him" (Matthew 3:17). The words seem to be a blend of two Old Testament texts, Isaiah 42:1 and Psalm 2:7, evidence that the early Christian community's own reflection on the meaning of Jesus and his mission is at work here. But the insistence on sonship, on the intimate bond between the Father and Jesus, begins a theme that is a hallmark of Jesus' religious experience. This privileged and warm relationship between Jesus and his Father finds no parallel in the Judaism of Jesus' day; it must be seen as a major motif of the Gospel portrait of Jesus.

The other prayers of the Gospel echo this motif. We

have two examples of Jesus' own personal prayer in the synoptic Gospels. The prayers of Jesus on the cross are put aside for the moment because they are quotations of a psalm. But in Matthew 11:25ff., we have a prayer of Jesus that bursts suddenly into the narrative: "Father, Lord of heaven and earth, to you I offer praise; for what you have hidden from the learned and the clever you have revealed to the merest children. Father, it is true. You have graciously willed it so. Everything has been given over to me by my Father. No one knows the Son but the Father, and no one knows the Father but the Son and anyone to whom the Son wishes to reveal him" (Matthew 11:25-27).

This text has baffled commentators. Its tone and cadence differ from the usual patterns of Matthew's Gospel. Its almost poetic style suggests that it may have been used as a liturgical hymn or prayer prior to its inclusion in the Gospel. But the effort to discover the meaning of the prayer's form does not negate its authentic ring. The emphasis on the intimate bond between Jesus and his Father and the address of God as "Father" are peculiar to Jesus.

These same unique features characterize the other important example of Jesus' prayer. All four Gospels provide us with the extraordinary picture of Jesus struggling in prayer as his death approaches. In the synoptic Gospels, the scene is the garden on the Mount of Olives. In John, the prayer is located at the end of Jesus' public ministry immediately before the Passover meal (12:27-28). Mark's wording brings us closest to the original form. Jesus addresses God not simply as "Father" but with the Aramaic word *Abba* (14:36): "Abba, you have the power to do all things. Take this cup away from me. But let it be as you would have it, not as I."

The use of *Abba* could have entered the Gospel tradition only because Jesus used it. The ordinary word for "father" in Aramaic and Hebrew is *ab*. *Abba* is an intimate diminutive, almost like "Dad" or "Daddy" in English. A rabbinic text says that "when a child experiences the taste of wheat, it learns to say *abba* and *imma* (mommy)." But the word was not used only by small children. Texts have been found where adults use the term *abba* as an expression of intimacy and affection for their father. But there is no parallel in Judaism for its use as an address in prayer to God. No text, either in the Old Testament or in rabbinic writings, ever dared to address Yahweh in such familiar terms. The first example of it ever found in Jewish circles is from a medieval prayer from southern Italy.

Judaism's reverence for its God needs little demonstration. Every page of its sacred book breathes awe and respect for the name of Yahweh. The divine name was not even to be pronounced by human lips. Alternates such as *adonai*, "my Lord," or a wide selection of euphemisms were used in its place. As in many religions, God was thought of as a father by Judaism. Some of the most beautiful texts of the Old Testament, such as Jeremiah 31:20, attribute to Yahweh the loving concern that a father has for his children: "Is Ephraim my dear son? Is he my darling child? . . . Therefore my heart yearns for him; I must have mercy on him, says the Lord." But the warmth of this concept did not allow an Israelite the presumption of addressing Yahweh directly as "my Father" in prayer.

Jesus' prayer stands as unique against this background of strict reverence. Some scholars suggest that *Abba* was the way Jesus habitually referred to his Father. The many texts that have Jesus refer to God as "my Father" or "your Father" may reflect the nearest the Greek translations could come to the original sense of the Aramaic without resorting to a simple transliteration, as the text of Mark 14:36 does. In any case, it cannot be doubted that Jesus' reference to God as Father reveals his intimate relationship to God.

Equally striking is the fact that this intimacy of Jesus with his Father becomes part of the Christian heritage. The Lord's Prayer, the prayer that Matthew and Luke trace to Jesus' own instruction, makes this clear. "This is how you are to pray: Our Father in heaven . . ." (Matthew 6:9; Luke 11:2). Twice in Paul the unique Christian address of God as *Abba* is testified to: "You did not receive a spirit of slavery leading you back into fear, but a spirit of adoption through which we cry out, 'Abba' (that is, 'Father')" (Romans 8:15). "The proof that you are sons is the fact that God has sent forth into our hearts the spirit of his Son which cries out 'Abba!' ('Father!')" (Galatians 4:6). The presence of the Aramaic *abba* in both of these Pauline texts can be explained only by the fact that they witness to a tradition of prayer originating with Jesus himself. Thus Jesus' intimate relationship to his Father became one of his greatest gifts to his disciples.

Here, in this confident, intimate bond between Jesus and his Father, is the secret of Jesus' zeal. So much of his preaching and teaching derive their freshness and appeal from this sense of kinship. To conceive of God as "his Father" did not mean for Jesus that Yahweh was simply the originator of the universe. Jesus understood "Father" in affectionate terms. God was "Father" because this term best described the compelling, nourishing love that Jesus himself experienced. We do not have to speculate about this; some of the most memorable of Jesus' parables and sayings reveal the touching dimensions of God's fatherly love.

Most of Jesus' conception of God as Father centers on the tireless, healing love of God for his children. His love is gratuitous, indiscriminate, lavish. Jesus' parable of the Prodigal Son is perhaps the most eloquent example. It is so familiar that we may have to make an effort to appreciate the extraordinary conception of divine love that it illustrates. That conception is rooted in Jesus' own experience of his Father. The story is multidimensional, focusing first on the younger son as he squanders his patrimony and then repents and later on the grumbling of the older son. But the central figure of the parable is the father. He doles out the son's inheritance without question. It is the son's conviction that his father will forgive that brings him home. The father runs to meet the prodigal, throwing his arms around him and kissing him, preparing a great feast to celebrate his return.

Chapter 20 of Matthew's Gospel records the parable of the Laborers in the Vineyard. The Kingdom is compared to the owner of the vineyard who hires workmen for his vineyard. Throughout the day, different groups are hired: at dawn, midmorning, noon, midafternoon, and even late afternoon. When the work is finished, the laborers line up to receive their pay, beginning with those hired last. When the workers hired at dawn come forward, they are shocked to find that they receive no more than those hired late in the day. Their anger seems perfectly reasonable: "This last group did only an hour's work, but you have put them on the same basis as us who have worked a full day in the scorching heat." The parable is not meant to illustrate social justice; its message is that the Father's generosity exceeds all human expectations: ". . . are you envious because I am generous?"

This insistence on the extravagance of the Father's merciful love is complemented by several parables and sayings that reflect on the sheer joy and delight of the Father over a sinner who repents. He is like the shepherd who leaves the 99 to search after the one lost sheep. "And when he finds it, he puts it on his shoulders in jubilation. Once arrived home, he invites friends and neighbors in and says to them, 'Rejoice with me because I have found my lost sheep.' I tell you, there will likewise be more joy in heaven over one repentant sinner than over ninety-nine righteous people who have no need to repent" (Luke 15:4-7). Or he is like the woman who loses one silver coin. When she finds it, "she calls in her friends and neighbors to say, 'Rejoice with me! I have found the silver piece I lost.' I tell you, there will be the same kind of joy before the angels of God over one repentant sinner" (Luke 15:8-10).

A love that is overwhelmingly generous, forgiving, tolerant, a love that finds sheer delight in reconciliation —these are the tender ways whereby Jesus defines his awareness of God as Father. And this kind of love defines Jesus' own ministry of healing and teaching.

Jesus as Teacher

At the center of Jesus' consciousness was the experience of God as Father. The urgency of Jesus' mission was to proclaim that this God is near. Thus life in the Kingdom implies a new awareness of our relationship to God—or put more accurately, God's relationship to us. But it does not stop there. The coming of the Kingdom also implies a new relationship of man to man. Jesus did not simply announce the Kingdom; he taught its implications for living.

"Teacher" is one of the most characteristic titles of Jesus in the Gospels. In fact, he is called "teacher" more than anything else. The word appears over 50 times in the Gospels; of these, 30 are applied directly to Jesus. But the Gospels also insist that Jesus was not a teacher in the sense commonly accepted in his day. The rabbis were teachers, as we have discussed. They carefully transmitted to their disciples the religious heritage of Israel—a knowledge of the Torah and the network of oral traditions that developed in an effort to make the Torah applicable to ordinary life. Because the rabbis were the transmitters of a heritage, the authority of the past was crucial. A rabbinic interpretation had weight if it could be fortified by the support of traditional rabbinic opinion, the "authority of the fathers."

But Jesus' own statements are decidedly different. He never cites the authority of other rabbis to bolster what he says. Even his citations of Scripture appear as mere confirmation or illustration of what he declares rather than as clinching proof. Jesus' words are their own authority. Their source is his own perception. He was not a debater.

The truth is laid before the listener with compelling simplicity—either to be accepted or rejected.

Scholars point to a fascinating hallmark of many of Jesus' more solemn statements. They often begin, "Amen, amen I say to you . . ." The Hebrew word *amen* normally means "certainly." It is used in the Old Testament and Hebrew literature as a response to a benediction or to an oath, much like the use of "amen" in English today. But Jesus uses the word as a confirmation of *his own* statements, a usage without parallel in Jewish literature. Many scholars believe that the expression is a substitute for the phrase used by many of the Old Testament prophets to introduce their messages: "Thus says the Lord." Jesus' "Amen, amen I say to you" rings with awesome authority. The same tone is present in Matthew's Sermon on the Mount when Jesus contrasts his own teaching with traditional interpretations: "You have heard it said . . . but I say to you." The brisk and convincing authority of Jesus is reflected too in the amazed reaction of the crowds that punctuates many of his Gospel discourses: "Jesus finished this discourse and left the crowds spellbound at his teaching. The reason was that he taught with authority and not like their scribes" (Matthew 7:29).

Jesus' commanding presence was not based on an inflated ego; it derived from the strength of his own insight and conviction. The heart of that insight, we have been contending, was Jesus' own experience of God as a loving Father. The Gospels do no offer us a neat, well-organized presentation of this teaching. Jesus' instructions are mostly "on the run": occasional stories or parables; conversations with his disciples; sharp, brief conflicts with his opponents. Even the infrequent, longer discourses, such as the Sermon on the Mount in chapters 5 to 7 of Matthew, or the discourses of John's Gospel, are not logically patterned presentations. They are, for the most part, compositions of the evangelists who have gathered isolated sayings of Jesus into loose collections. Thus the reader must sift through all of the sayings of Jesus to catch the spirit of his teaching. Not everything he says can be reduced to a single theme or guiding idea. But Jesus' insight into the indiscriminate love of his Father provides the ultimate key to practically every word the Gospels record.

There can be little doubt that love—love of God and love of neighbor—is the center of Jesus' instructions. Each of the evangelists testifies to this love, although in varying ways. The three synoptic Gospels provide a scene in which Jesus is asked, "Which is the greatest commandment of the law?" Matthew and Mark place the scene at the conclusion of Jesus' career, during his final days in Jerusalem (Matthew 22:34-40; Mark 12:28-34). In Luke's account, a similar discussion occurs in the midst of Jesus' ministry (Luke 10:25-28) as he moves on his long journey from Galilee through Samaria towards Jerusalem.

In each case, the question posed to Jesus is typical of rabbinic debate. Rabbis often discussed how the 613 commandments of the Torah could be summarized in one neat injunction. Jesus' reply draws on two major Old Testament citations: 1- love of God as expressed in Deuteronomy 6:5, "You shall love the Lord your God with your whole heart, with your whole soul, and with all your mind," and 2- love of neighbor as expressed in Leviticus 19:18, "You shall love your neighbor as yourself." In Luke's account, the lawyer who puts the question to Jesus ends up by answering his own question (Luke 10:27).

Some remarkable features of this discussion should not be overlooked. The formulation of Jesus' response is not novel; it is a quotation from the Old Testament. Even the response of summarizing the Law under these two great commandments is not without parallel in Jewish literature. The unique note is insistence on the unity of these two commands and the contention that they are the basis of interpretation for *all* of the Law. *Both* commands are in response to the opening question "Which is the greatest?"

This is particularly clear in Luke's rendition where the enumeration "first" and "second" is dropped and the two commands have been completely sealed into one. And each of the evangelists adds a unique emphasis of his own to the words of Jesus to insist on the paramount position of the love command. In Mark's conversation, the scribe who put the question to Jesus is impressed at the response he receives: "Excellent, Teacher! You are right in saying, 'He is the One, there is no other than he.' Yes, 'to love him with all our heart, with all our thoughts and with all our strength, and to love our neighbor as ourselves' is worth more than any burnt offering or sacrifice." The Gospel goes on to comment: "Jesus approved the insight of this answer and told him, 'You are not far from the Kingdom of God'" (Mark 12:32-34). This exchange stresses the primacy of the love command over the sacred obligations of the Temple cult. In Matthew's version, Jesus himself adds the following closing comment: "On these two commandments the whole law is based, and the prophets as well" (22:40). The "Law" and the "prophets" were the two great divisions of the books of the Old Testament at the time of Jesus. Thus Jesus' words insist that the love command is the fundamental principle for interpreting the entire Law. Such concern with the place of the Law within the teaching of Jesus is a typical emphasis of Matthew's Jewish-Christian Gospel.

Both Matthew and Mark seem to hold the discussion of the love command to a certain theoretical level. Luke's practical emphasis savors more of Jesus' own style. Coming up with the right answer to the question of the greatest commandment of the Law is no longer the prime issue; living it out is. This shift in emphasis, an emphasis echoed in most of Jesus' other sayings about love, is apparent in the way Luke presents the scene in chapter 10 of his Gospel. A lawyer asks, "Teacher, what must I do to inherit everlasting life?" Jesus turns the question on the lawyer: "What is written in the law? How do you read it?"

The lawyer's response is correct; he cites the twofold command of love of God and neighbor (now neatly joined into one). The subsequent response of Jesus seems almost impatient with the discussion: "You have answered correctly. Do this and you shall live." The answer is almost too simple, too straightforward. The lawyer has asked how he is to gain life, and the teacher of Nazareth has unmasked the questioner's lack of seriousness by proving that the lawyer already knew the answer. Unwilling to appear outmaneuvered, the lawyer attempts to throw some complexity into the discussion: "And who is my neighbor?" At this point, the genius of Luke's presentation becomes apparent. Now fused onto the discussion of the twofold commandment of love is Jesus' parable of the Good Samaritan. A Samaritan, detested in the eyes of any law-abiding Jew, demonstrates the law of love by a practical response to someone in need. The priest and the Levite, paragons of Israelite virtue, fail the same test.

The conclusion of the parable touches the heart of the matter. Jesus actually refuses to answer the lawyer's question, "Who is my neighbor?" The question now is: "Which of these three, in your opinion, was neighbor to the man who fell in with the robbers?" The perspective has been reversed. The lawyer, in effect, has asked about the limits of the love command: Who is my neighbor? That is, to whom am I bound to show compassion and love? Jesus centers on the response itself. The "limits" of love can never be defined by any theoretical projection. The command of love is never circumscribed by the nationality, status, or inherent lovableness of the potential "neighbor." The neighbor, the one who has a claim on my love, is anyone in need to whom I am able to respond.

This insistence on the absolutely indiscriminate nature of love within the Kingdom is the dominant perspective of almost all of Jesus' teaching. Here the reader of the Gospel can hear the authentic voice of Jesus of Nazareth. If any saying of the Gospel can claim to be an unaltered saying of

Jesus, it is his statement on love of enemies. Virtually every New Testatment scholar, Christian and Jewish, traces this unique command to Jesus himself. It has no parallel in rabbinic or biblical texts, nor is it found in any of the aphorisms of Greek or Roman culture.

The saying is found in the Gospels of Matthew and Luke in similar if not identical settings. Both evangelists have placed the saying in one of Jesus' long discourses. For Matthew, this is the Sermon on the Mount; in Luke's Gospel, Jesus' Sermon on the Plain. Both evangelists immerse the saying in a series of "antitheses" or contrasts where Jesus distances his own teaching from the traditional teaching of Judaism. In Matthew, the command to love the enemy is the climax of a series of six masterful, antithetical sayings (cf. Matthew 5:21-48); in Luke, the same command begins the series of antithetical sayings. For purposes of illustration, we concentrate on Matthew's presentation, although both evangelists offer practically the same wording.

"You have heard the commandment, 'You shall love your countryman but hate your enemy.' My command to you is: love your enemies, pray for your persecutors" (Matthew 5:43-44). The commandment, "Love your country men but hate your enemy," had been the cause of some consternation among biblical scholars. All other commands that Jesus cites in this section of the Gospel as being representative of the type of response permissible under the old Law but now superseded by his own can be traced either to the Old Testament or to the teaching of the rabbis. But no parallel could be found for the command to "hate your enemy." Not until the discovery of the Dead Sea Scrolls at the Qumran monastery was evidence available to justify Jesus' statement. Many of these Jewish sectarian writings contain statements such as: "Love all the sons of light, each according to his lot among the council of God, but . . . hate all the sons of darkness, each according to his guilt in the vengeance of God." This and similar texts from the Qumran community testify to a sectarian attitude that encouraged love among the members of the community ("the sons of light") but counseled hatred for gentiles and those who did not keep the Law in its purity ("the sons of darkness").

Jesus' command to "love your enemy" directly affronts a sectarian attitude prevalent in his own times. We find here the same spirit evidenced in the Good Samaritan parable. Love must be indiscriminate. Who is the enemy? The verses that follow the love command spell out in prosaic terms the meaning of "enemy": Pray for your persecutors; do good to those who hate you; bless those who curse you; turn the other cheek; give your shirt to someone who takes your coat; give to those who persistently beg and borrow. Jesus does not give us the luxury of loving only the remote enemy whose hostility diminishes with distance. The "enemy" in the teaching of Jesus turns out to be as near and as ordinary as the persistent borrower.

The foundation for these compelling demands of Jesus brings us back to his own experience of God. To love your enemy, Jesus states (Matthew 5:45), "will prove that you are sons of your heavenly Father, for his sun rises on the just and the unjust. If you love those who love you, what merit is there in that? Do not tax collectors do as much? And if you greet your brothers only, what is so praiseworthy about that? Do not pagans do as much? In a word, you must be made perfect as your heavenly Father is perfect."

The same penetrating insight into God's love for all his children—bad and good, responsive and hostile—fires Jesus' conviction about what the quality of life is to be in the Kingdom. To be a disciple, and thus different from the unconverted pagan, means being as the heavenly Father is: "perfect." Luke uses the word "merciful" (Luke 6:36). Both terms can be reduced to the same reality. For "perfect" in Matthew's context means "whole," "complete." To be whole or complete, as the Father is complete, means loving with his limitless compassion. The word "perfect" is used only one other time in Matthew's Gospel. In Matthew 19:21, the rich young man is told that if he wishes to become "perfect," he must give his possessions to the poor and follow Jesus. Following Jesus in his ministry of compassion defines the meaning of being "perfect as your heavenly Father is perfect."

Not too many of Jesus' other sayings explicitly refer to love. Jesus seems uninterested in parading the word. The reality of human love is defined more realistically in other terms: "forgiveness," "reconciliation," "avoidance of judgment," "compassion." Our own experience tells us that human love is not lived to a lyrical beat but comes to awkward expression in our fumbling efforts to bind up wounds, to restore friendship, to make amends. It is testimony to the genuiness of Jesus' own humanity that his teaching on love is couched in such sober terms. These muted urgings to love flood the Gospels.

Reconciliation is the byword of the Kingdom. "If you bring your gift to the altar and there recall that your brother has anything against you, leave your gift at the altar, go first to be reconciled with your brother, and then come and offer your gift" (Matthew 5:24). The disciples are to bind up the wounds of hostility as quickly as possible, even if it means settling with an opponent on the way to the courtroom (Matthew 5:25). To "grow angry with your brother" or to use abusive language will be held answerable in the Kingdom (Matthew 5:22).

The art of forgiving tests the genuiness of one's relationship to God. The prayer of the Kingdom includes this key petition: "forgive us the wrong we have done as we forgive those who wrong us" (Matthew 6:12). In Matthew's Gospel, the words of Jesus immediately following the prayer center on this very theme: "If you forgive the faults of others, your heavenly Father will forgive you yours. If you do not forgive others, neither will your Father forgive you" (Matthew 6:14-15).

This theme of reciprocity courses through many of

Jesus' sayings on the practical implications of the love command. It seems to ask: How can we claim to be a son or daughter of the heavenly Father if we do not appreciate the quality of his love for us, a love that is boundless in forgiveness? To fashion love into something other than this is to turn one's back on the Father of mercies. So if the disciple wishes to avoid this "self judgment," he must stop passing judgment on his brother. "Your verdict on others will be the verdict passed on you. The measure with which you measure will be used to measure you. Why look at the speck in your brother's eye when you miss the plank in your own? How can you say to your brother, 'Let me take that speck out of your eye,' while all the time the plank remains in your own?" (Matthew 7:1-5).

The love command, then, becomes translated into an unlimited call for forgiveness. This fundamental teaching of Jesus finds no clearer expression than in chapter 18 of Matthew's Gospel. The evangelist has fashioned a number of Jesus' sayings and parables into a discourse on the quality of life in the Kingdom. At the climax of the discourse, Peter comes forward with a question: "Lord, when my brother wrongs me, how often must I forgive him? Seven times?" There seems to be a gentle irony here. Poor Peter must have been somewhat proud of himself. To suggest forgiveness to a limit of seven borders on magnanimity. Some rabbinic texts set the limit at four offenses. But Jesus' reply shatters even Peter's generous limits: "No, not seven times: I say, seventy times seven times." The number has been multiplied into infinity. In the book of Genesis, Lamech boasts that any injury to him will be avenged "seventy times seven" (Genesis 4:24). But with Jesus, the call becomes one of unlimited forgiveness.

Jesus immediately appends a parable to this statement about forgiveness. It is a perfect illustration of how insight into God's love for us becomes the norm for our love of each other. In the parable of the Merciless Official, a king decides to check his accounts. He discovers that one of his aides owes him an enormous debt. Confronted, the servant throws himself before this master and begs for mercy: "My Lord, be patient with me and I will pay you back in full." The response of the king is the key to the parable: "Moved with pity, the master let the official go and wrote off the debt." But the servant forgiven his debt is untouched by his master's mercy. "But when that same official went out he met a fellow servant who owed him a mere fraction of what he himself owed. He seized him and throttled him. 'Pay back what you owe!' " When his fellow servant pleads for mercy, the official "would hear none of it, instead he had him put in jail until he paid back what he owed."

The other servants of the household are distressed by this callous behavior, and they report the official to the king. The master immediately summons the merciless official and condemns him for his lack of forgiveness: "You worthless wretch! I canceled your entire debt when you pleaded with me. Should you not have dealt mercifully with your fellow servant, as I dealt with you?" Outraged, the master hands him over to the torturers until he pays back all that he owes. Jesus' conclusion summarizes the very heart of his teaching: "My heavenly Father will treat you in exactly the same way unless each of you forgives his brother from his heart" (Matthew 18:35).

Jesus and the Law

Jesus' insistence that love—love expressed in a practical response to a situation of need—was the essence of religious fidelity put him at odds with the Judaism of his day. Not that love of God and love of neighbor were not central concerns of the believing Jew. Anyone who has read the Bible cannot accept the too-common stereotype that labels the Old Testament as a religion of justice and the New Testament as a religion of love and mercy. As we have seen, the very words of Jesus' love command are citations of Hebrew Scripture.

The conflict between Jesus and his fellow Jewish teachers originated on a more subtle basis. Rabbinic Judaism ascribed to love as the meaning of religious fidelity. But the dimensions of love were carefully circumscribed by the prescriptions of the Law. If a man could be faithful to all of the detailed demands of the Law, then he could be confident that he had "loved." He could be sure that he was doing what God asked of him if he adhered to ritual regulations, if he observed the Sabbath laws, if he performed the proper prayers and sacrifices.

Jesus' teaching views the relationship between men and God from a fundamentally different perspective. It was not a case of his rejecting the Law as useless or harmful. Nor did he hold in contempt the Pharisees' efforts to make the Law applicable to everyday life. But, as the famous British scholar C. H. Dodd says, the angle at which Jesus' teaching touches life is different. True fidelity to God, genuine religion, can be nothing less than a full, loving response to God and to neighbor. Here is the center that judges all else, prescriptions of the Law included. True fidelity can never be measured by how many laws we have kept. Its only test is the quality of our love.

Jesus' approach to religious fidelity was not defined in the abstract but in the realm of decision. Here his basic conflict with the Pharisees and other exponents of the Law becomes clear. One of the most sacred obligations of the Jew was to keep "holy the Sabbath," to observe the Sabbath rest. This religious custom, more than any other, distinguished Jew from gentile. By means of their oral interpretation of the Law, the rabbis had developed a complicated network of prescriptions that spelled out exactly how the Sabbath was to be kept. The original purpose of the Sabbath, a moment of genuine rest and peace in the midst of man's creative toil, became smothered in a blanket of detailed regulations that attempted to cover every contingency of the Sabbath day—how far one could walk, how to prepare one's meals, and so on.

Several Gospel incidents record Jesus' instinctive reaction to this stifling legalism. Jesus would observe the Sabbath regulations—but not when they formed a barrier to the demands of love and compassion. His basic principle cuts through the overbearing formalism of the rabbinic laws: "The sabbath was made for man, not man for the sabbath" (Mark 2:27). Thus he would cure sickness and alleviate hunger despite the constant accusing eyes of the Pharisees (cf. Mark 3:1). "Is it permitted to do a good deed on the sabbath—or an evil one? To preserve life—or destroy it?" But the legalism of his opponents insulates them from the penetrating truth of Jesus' words. Their only response was to begin to plot how they might destroy him (Mark 3:6).

Other aspects of rabbinic law draw a similar response from Jesus. The thirst for ritual purity spawned a host of regulations designed to protect the believer from anyone or anything that might defile him in the eyes of God. Certain foods were to be avoided. Numerous ritual washings were performed daily. Contact with gentiles and those ignorant of the Law was not permitted. Jesus' response again cuts against the very grain of Jewish legal tradition: "Hear me, all of you, and try to understand. Nothing that enters a man from outside can make him impure; that which comes out of him, and only that, constitutes impurity" (Mark 7:14-15). One's own integrity, the active response of love and compassion, defines true purity in the eyes of God rather than attempts to maintain external purity.

The demand for wholeness and integrity approaches the heart of Jesus' critique of the rabbinic Law. The Law itself does not cripple fidelity, but the almost inevitable spin-offs that accompany a legalistic morality do. The attempt to define fidelity as a specific set of rules seems doomed to end up substituting the rules for the fidelity they are meant to foster. Externalism, formalism, and an infectious pride in one's own accomplishment subvert the very purpose of the Law; they cripple the believer's ability to respond to the situation with compassion and love.

Many of Jesus' strongest sayings lash out at this frame of mind. "You have made a fine art of setting aside God's commandment in the interests of keeping your traditions" (Mark 7:9). "You pay tithes on mint and herbs and seeds while neglecting the weightier matters of the law, justice and mercy and good faith. It is these you should have practiced, without neglecting the others" (Mark 23:23).

Prayer, fasting, and almsgiving must be utterly sincere. "When you are praying, do not behave like the hypocrites who love to stand and pray in synagogues or on street corners in order to be noticed. I give you my word, close your door, and pray to your Father in private. Then your Father, who sees what no man sees, will repay you" (Matthew 6:5-6). "When you fast, you are not to look glum as the hypocrites do. They change the appearance of their faces so that others may see they are fasting. I assure you, they are already repaid. When you fast, see to it that you groom your hair and wash your face. In that way no one can see you are fasting but your Father who is hidden; and your Father who sees what is hidden will repay you" (Matthew 6:16-18). "When you give alms, for example, do not blow a horn before you in synagogues and streets like hypocrites looking for applause. You can be sure of this much, they are already repaid. In giving alms you are not to let your left hand know what your right hand is doing. Keep your deeds of mercy secret, and your Father who sees in secret will repay you" (Matthew 6:2-4).

Speech and action, like prayer, must proceed from an inner response. There is no need for the disciple to swear oaths to reinforce the truth of what he says, as the rabbis constantly did. "Say, 'Yes' when you mean 'Yes' and 'No' when you mean 'No.' Anything beyond that is from the evil one" (Matthew 5:37).

As mentioned earlier, there is little doubt that some of the edge in these sayings reflects the later hostility that existed between the synagogue and the young Christian church. But if the language has been altered, the basic thrust of Jesus' teaching has not. For Jesus, every response, every decision, every action had to proceed from love. This defined the meaning of integrity. Jesus' insistence on love and compassion as well as his revulsion to legalism and hypocrisy ultimately find their authority in his knowledge of his Father. It was the Father's love for his children that opened to Jesus the meaning of human love. It was the Father's love that was showered on the good and the bad, that wrote off the debt, that searched out the lost, that rejoiced in repentance, that demanded the weightier laws of justice, mercy, and compassion. Jesus' experience of the love of his Father, his *Abba,* is the source of his teaching.

Throughout our discussion of Jesus' teaching, we have rarely appealed to the Gospel of John. John's Gospel, more than the others, has brought Christian interpretation to bear on the tradition of Jesus' words and deeds. John presents Jesus as the revelation of the Father. He is the Eternal Word who speaks the Father's name. To see Jesus is to see the Father. Jesus, by word and work, reveals the infinite love of the Father for his children. He is "light" for those in darkness, "bread" for the hungry, "living water" for those who thirst, the "way" for those who are lost, "truth" for the perplexed, "life" and "resurrection" for those who taste death. These basic images are used by John to identify Jesus as the revealer of the Father to those who believe. In the magnificent last discourse of Jesus, John lays out the very core of the teaching of Jesus:

As the Father has loved me, so I have loved you. Live on in my love. You will live in my love if you keep my commandments, even as I have kept my Father's commandments and live in his love. All this I tell you that my joy may be yours and your joy may be complete. This is my commandment: love one another as I have loved you" (John 15:9-12).

111

The teaching of Jesus savors of the same freshness and unique authority that we discovered in his dealings with his friends. No church, no evangelist, no accident of time and culture could create a man or a message like this. To listen carefully to these words is to draw close to the Jesus of the Gospels.

Chapter 5

Jesus Heals

The Gospel portrait of Jesus would not be accurate or complete if our image of him were that of a mere teacher or dispenser of religious truth. A great deal of the Gospel material concentrates not on what Jesus says but on what he does—his miracles of healing, of exorcism, of power over the forces of nature.

The four evangelists are unanimous on this point. Mark has Jesus begin his ministry with a burst of healing activity in the lake town of Capernaum: a raving maniac is cured in the synagogue itself, Simon's mother-in-law is cured of a fever in her home, a leper is touched and cleansed, the paralytic is able to walk again, a man with a withered hand has it restored. And by means of several rapid summaries, Mark indicates that these are only a few examples of Jesus' healing activity: "Because he had cured many, all who had afflictions kept pushing toward him to touch him. Unclean spirits would catch sight of him, fling themselves down at his feet, and shout, 'You are the Son of God!' " (3:10-11). The crush of the crowds becomes so great that Jesus takes the precaution of having a boat ready for escape. And when Jesus' family hears of his frenzied pace—he is not even stopping to eat—their good sense tells them that he is "out of his mind," and they set out to rescue him from this nonsense (Mark 3:21).

Matthew has schematized the healing activity of Jesus, but the impression of a man consumed with his mission of healing is scarcely different from that of Mark's Gospel. In a masterful summary placed at the very beginning of Jesus' public ministry, Matthew notes: "Jesus toured all of Galilee. He taught in their synagogues, proclaimed the good news of the kingdom, and cured the people of every disease and illness. As a consequence of this, his reputation traveled the length of Syria. They carried to him all those afflicted with various diseases and racked with pain: the possessed, the lunatics, the paralyzed. He cured them all" (4:23-24). In chapters 8 and 9 of his Gospel, Matthew lays out a string of 10 miracles, absorbing the same incidents mentioned by Mark. And, as did his predecessor, the evangelist injects several summaries to indicate that the miracles recorded are only samples of Jesus' widespread healing activity.

The story is much the same in Luke and in John. Luke prefaces Jesus' public ministry with a quotation from Isaiah 61: "The spirit of the Lord is upon me; therefore, he has anointed me. He has sent me to bring glad tidings to the poor, to proclaim liberty to captives, recovery of sight to the blind and release to prisoners, to announce a year of favor from the Lord" (Luke 4:18-19). That keynote text, dramatically read in Jesus' home synagogue of Nazareth, presages Jesus' ministry of healing activity among the poor. Throughout Luke's Gospel, Jesus reaches out to heal the sick, to expel demons, to raise the dead. John is more sparing of miracles in his Gospel, but they have a special place of prominence in Jesus' ministry. Seven great "signs" mark the first half of the Gospel, covering the entirety of Jesus' public mission. Several of these "signs" or miracles become the occasion for Jesus' long discourses, so characteristic of the fourth Gospel.

Thus all of our sources are in agreement: Jesus was a miracle worker. The same testimony is born out by the book of Acts, which refers to Jesus as a "man whom God sent to you with miracles, wonders, and signs as his credentials" (2:22). Even rabbinic texts remember Jesus as a "sorcerer" and a wonder worker. To round out our Gospel portrait of Jesus, we need to examine this substantial portion of Gospel material devoted to Jesus' miracles to discover what it might tell us about the healer.

The Meaning of Miracle

Almost every modern treatment of the miracles of Jesus is prefaced with some agonizing over the problem that the very notion of miracle poses for the contemporary mind. Our own discussion is no different. No matter how religious we might be, we are products of our own world. And a basic tenet of the world view that most of us share is an expectation that all of physical reality is ultimately explainable on its own terms. If there are footprints, then someone has walked by. If there is drought, then atmospheric conditions, no matter how complex, have caused it. If there is sickness, then we must find the virus. We harbor our share of myths and superstitions, just as every age of mankind has done; but in theory, we hold that every observable phenomenon has an explaining cause, even if for the moment it eludes us.

For most citizens of the 20th century, a "miracle" is by definition some phenomenon that ruptures the explanatory link between cause and effect. It is an exception, a violation of the "laws of nature" whereby something occurs whose cause is outside the world of physical reality. Very few of us have ever witnessed something that we would confidently call a miracle in the strict sense, even though we may have prayed earnestly for one and believed that God was capable of working one. Certainly few of us have come across the steady performance of miracles such as the Gospels almost routinely attribute to Jesus. Thus when modern man turns to the pages of the New Testament to read of wonders attributed to Jesus, stirrings of scepticism are understandable. At least some effort is needed to fit Jesus' activity into our own miracle-less experience.

115

Not all of the distance between the Gospel's world view and our own can be neatly bridged. The Gospels' insistence that Jesus performed miraculous deeds, even to the point of "breaking the laws of nature," ultimately can be answered either by choosing to dismiss the testimony of the Gospel tradition or by believing that Jesus was no ordinary man. But some refinements can and should be made before that choice is too blatantly forced on the modern mind. A responsible understanding of Jesus' world and of what "miracle" meant to it helps bring the Gospel tradition closer to our own experience.

First, we should be aware that the biblical mind was unlikely to define a miracle the way that we do. For us, it is an exception, a rupture of the observable order of the world that we experience and that science works to explain. But a believer of the first century did not think of it in these terms. A "miracle" understood as a manifestation of God's control over the world that he had made really was not an "exception"; rather, it was a vivid insight into the way things actually were. God directly controlled his creation. He shaped man's fate, and he ruled the awesome forces of nature. If God chose to manifest his control over life in a clearly visible way, that was no violation of any law but a wonderful sign of the power that normally effected men in more subtle and ordinary ways. Thus the exceptional thing about miracles was not their possibility but their manifestation. A miracle provoked awe and reverence, even fear, but not fundamental surprise.

Given biblical man's view of the universe, it is not unexpected that he would be likely to discover "miracles" in his world much more frequently than we might in ours. The modern believer considers creation as autonomous, existing, and developing according to its own inner elements and patterns. Man as a part of creation is destined to discover its secrets and harness its energies. If some phenomenon eclipses our experience, then we must strive to uncover its explanation hidden in the richness of created reality. But the biblical mind might not be tempted to pursue the search into the mysteries of created reality with our conviction. A cogent explanation was near at hand. A baffling illness, a sudden cure, the fearsome power of a storm, the inevitable pattern of the seasons—all of these experiences were signposts that supernatural powers touched the everyday life of man. Thus miracles and miracle workers were much more commonplace in the first century than they are in the 20th century. Many rabbis, contemporaries of Jesus, were considered wonder workers, able to cure illness and to check the forces of evil through Yahweh's power. But miracle working was not confined to Palestine or Judaism. Many of the Greek religions boasted their own miracle makers, and other regions of the Middle Eastern world experienced similar occurrences.

If the first-century believer was convinced of the reality of miracles, he was convinced too of the *need* for miracles. Man's vulnerability was much more apparent to ancient man than it is to us. Medicine was, of course, still primitive. Hospitals for the mentally ill were unknown. The blind, the lame, the lepers (a term covering a host of skin diseases), and the psychotic were pushed into the backwash of normal society. Feared and avoided, they were repulsive proof of how mankind was a victim of forces that defied natural explanation. Here is an accurate picture of the background of the Gospel narrative: The blind and lame scattered along the roadside begging for coins from passersby; lepers, banned from town and temple, moving in condemned bands across the countryside; epileptics and psychotics roaming wild among the tombs or cruelly manacled, rolling on the ground and shrieking in uncontrolled lunacy. Jesus and his contemporaries faced the stark reality of sickness and death in a way that we seldom do.

Biblical reflection tended to tie together the vast array of ills that tortured man; all of them were labeled the work of evil. Sin, sickness, chaos, death were practically the same thing. Some strands of biblical tradition had taken the rather simplistic view that each manifestation of sickness and death could be traced to the responsibility of personal sin. So if someone were cut down by a tragic death or suffered from sickness, it was the result of some hidden sin committed by himself or at least by an ancestor. This was the case made to Job by his friends. But such a naive solution to the problem of suffering was rejected by wiser elements of biblical thought, as the author of Job himself so eloquently did. Death and suffering could not be written off as just payment for individual sin. The mystery of evil was far more complex and far more baffling. The truly innocent had to suffer as well as the guilty. Jesus too acknowledged the mystery of suffering when he refused the implication that the Galileans executed by Pilate were somehow responsible for their misfortune (Luke 13:2).

But if mature biblical reflection rejected the notion that all suffering could be explained by guilt for sin, it still clung to the notion that all the various forms of death men had to contend with were somehow part of a single mystery of evil. It made little difference whether someone was possessed by an evil spirit or was blind or was corrupted by leprosy or had seen the life of one's daughter snuffed out. All were manifestations of evil. All of them were blights on God's creation. All were enemies of God. And God's victory over evil would not be complete until all pain and suffering and death itself were overcome.

A miracle, understood as a visible manifestation of God's power over evil, was seen as a sign of that ultimate victory, assured but as yet incomplete, when God would rule his creation in power.

No doubt many of the phenomena considered miracles by Jesus' contemporaries would not be viewed as such by our own age. Perhaps many of the exorcisms performed by Jesus might be explained as the therapeutic effect of a compassionate and forceful personality on someone gripped by neurosis or hysteria. Many of his other cures might be "explained" in the same way. Many details and even some entire incidents recorded by the Gospels may have been inflated or even added as the Gospel tradition developed. But an honest appraisal of the Gospel material does not allow us to "solve" Jesus' miracles so easily. There still remains a solid residue of the tradition that insists that Jesus performed extraordinary signs of power over evil in its various forms. At this point, the question of faith moves forward to take a central place. But also at this point, a solid understanding of how miracles fit into Jesus' overall ministry and message becomes crucial. To become transfixed only by the questions of if and how Jesus worked miracles would be to miss the uniqueness of the Gospel portrait and the reason why miracles have such an important place within it.

Miracles and Ministry of the Kingdom

The key to understanding the purpose of the Gospel miracle tradition is Jesus' proclamation of the coming of God's Kingdom. We have noted how this basic theme guided the Gospel's selection of material when it describes Jesus' associations and his teaching. The same theme helps explain the importance given to miracles.

Jesus' searching of the Scriptures and his own experience in prayer had convinced him that the critical hour of the Kingdom was about to break onto the world. The God of the Kingdom, the Father of mercy and compassion, was drawing near to mankind in a way unprecedented in history. This fundamental conviction, based on Jesus' own intimate relationship to his Father, animated his teaching on love and forgiveness, and it provided the motivation for his sharp critique of Jewish legalism. It also drove Jesus to search out the poor and the outcasts, to bring to the alienated members of his own society the message of grace and reconciliation uniquely characteristic of this Galilean rabbi.

But Jesus' integrity is demonstrated by the fact that he was never content merely to proclaim and teach a message of love and mercy. His words and what he does are one. The herald of God's love and mercy becomes the healer of sickness and disease. The compassion that led him to seek out the poor and the afflicted drove him to cure them and to relieve their burdens. The Gospels leave little doubt that compassion was the motivation behind Jesus' healing ministry. Compassion urges Jesus to touch the leper and to cure him (Mark 1:41). Compassion for the crowd's hunger moves him to feed them. Compassion for their aimlessness and their affliction causes him to enlist the disciples in the same healing ministry (Matthew 9:36). Compassion for the widow of Naim leads Jesus to restore her son to life (Luke 7:13). Quite simply, Jesus cures because people are sick. In Matthew's Gospel, a challenge to Jesus' ministry among the poor and afflicted is turned back with a curt citation from the prophet Hosea: "People who are in good health do not need a doctor; sick people do. Go and learn the meaning of the words, 'It is mercy I desire and not sacrifice' " (Matthew 9:12-13).

But if compassion for those in need appears as an obvious motivation for Jesus' healing ministry, the Gospels make clear that this is not the total picture. Jesus is not painted simply as a humanitarian going about eradicating the ills of his society. The main emphasis of the Gospels, in fact, does not fall on this aspect of Jesus' healing ministry. Only when we look deeper into the Gospel picture does the full purpose of the miracle tradition become apparent.

The most characteristic designation applied to the miracles of Jesus in the Gospels is not "acts of kindness," nor even the technical Greek term for "miracle," but the word "power"—in Greek *dynamis*. Jesus' miracles are acts of power; they reveal the power of God himself working through Jesus. Several features of Jesus' miracles illustrate this Gospel emphasis.

The Gospels give special attention to Jesus' exorcisms, those acts of healing whereby Jesus liberates the victim from an evil spirit. Americans in recent years have been curious about the world of the occult. Fascination with witchcraft and exorcisms has spawned a number of pop religious sects and a record-breaking movie. But we should be careful not to equate too easily Jesus' exorcisms and our modern blend of superstition and put-on. A movie like *The Exorcist* subtly installs evil on the shelf of the fascinating and the improbable. It portrays a form of evil that may tingle our spines but, in fact, is completely remote from our ordinary experience. The biblical mind, however, acknowledged that the power of evil had nudged its way into daily life. The biblical mind linked sin and sickness and death as differing manifestations of the fundamental evil that inflicted man's world and set it in opposition to God. Personal responsibility for sin was not excused by allocating all evil to the arbitrary power of Satan, as much contemporary literature of the occult implies. The human contribution to sin and evil was accepted as a fact of life. At the same time, though, experience had convinced the Jew that the mystery of evil transcended individual choice; it could stifle the innocent as well as the guilty in its deathlike grip.

Jesus' confrontations with the manifestations of evil such as epilepsy or paralysis were merely skirmishes in an epic war. God's victory would be complete only when all evil—personal, communal, cosmic—was eradicated from his creation. This is the immense significance of Jesus' exorcisms. Jesus' power over Satan is a sign of God's saving power—a sign of the imminence of the Kingdom.

The Gospel temptation scenes dramatize this profound statement about Jesus. Mark (1:12-13) has Jesus driven into the desert immediately after his baptism. There he struggles with Satan, alone with the personification of evil in the traditional place where Israel was tested. This cryptic scene seems to symbolize the deeper meaning of

Jesus' approaching ministry. His healings, his teaching, his conflicts, even his death, are ultimately a confrontation between the power of God and the power of evil. Matthew and Luke have fortified the temptation scene with additional material. The struggle with Satan now becomes a dramatic dialogue: The prince of evil attempts to seduce God's Son from his ministry of the Kingdom. But Satan is defeated by the Son's obedience—again, a preview of the ultimate significance of Jesus' life.

What the temptation scenes symbolize, the exorcism stories dramatize in the prosaic setting of Jesus' ministry. During his public life, Jesus never directly confronts a disembodied Satan. The power of evil is manifested in human suffering: epileptics, paralytics, psychotics, poor tortured souls whose lives have been consumed by evil and despair. This is the tragic arena where Jesus confronts Satan. And, in each case, the power of God present in Jesus heals and restores. The man who roamed the cemetery of Gerasa is restored to his family (Mark 5:1-20). The epileptic boy is given back to his father (Mark 9:14-29). The mute speaks (Luke 11:14). The woman doubled over by a crippling spirit stands up straight and praises God (Luke 13:10-13). Mary Magdalene, liberated from the evil of lust, is free to follow Jesus and to minister to him (Luke 8:2).

Thus "exorcisms" in the Gospels are not a marketable superstition; they are a way of acknowledging the helplessness of humanity in the face of evil, an evil in which our own responsibility is not absent. The exorcism miracles become a strong statement about Jesus. His opponents themselves recognize the issue at stake. In a Gospel scene that undoubtedly is authentic, certain Pharisees interpret Jesus' power to cure as a sign of an alliance with Satan: "He is possessed by Beelzebul . . . He expels demons with the help of the prince of demons" (Mark 3:22). Jesus retorts that if this were so, then Satan's household must be divided; the work Jesus does is to overcome evil, not to advance it. He then adds a short parable (reported in all three synoptic Gospels) that reveals Jesus' own insight into his ministry. "No one can enter a strong man's house and despoil his property unless he has first put him under restraint. Only then can he plunder his house" (Mark 3:27). Jesus is a plunderer in Satan's own household, a man armed with the might of God who binds up the power of evil and rescues Satan's captives.

The exorcisms, therefore, are central to Jesus' ministry of the Kingdom. They are further signs of the unique authority and power of the Son; he reveals in what he says and does the compassionate love of the Father for his children. As Jesus tersely states: ". . . if it is by the finger of God that I cast out devils, then the reign of God is upon you" (Luke 11:20).

Jesus as the revelation of God's power to heal and to save is presented in even more dramatic fashion by the so-called "nature" miracles. These acts of power demonstrate Jesus' mastery over the very forces of creation—as, for example, in his stilling of the storm on the Lake of Galilee, or his walking on the water, or his feeding of the multitudes with only a few loaves and fishes. Included here might be the awesome power to bring back the dead, such as the daughter of Jairus or the son of the widow of Naim or Lazarus. Not all of the nature miracles are in a crisis situation. To satisfy the temple tax, Jesus directs Peter to retrieve a shekel coin from the mouth of a fish. On another occasion, the fig tree that does not bear fruit is cursed and it withers.

These miracles cause more difficult problems for the modern interpreter than any other aspect of the Gospel. The very term "nature miracle" does not come from the Gospels' own vocabulary; it is a category set up by exegetes who find that these incidents strain credibility more than the other accounts of Jesus' healing ministry.

For the Gospel tradition, however, all of these miracles had the same basic significance. Jesus' ability to cure blindness or to cast out an evil spirit really was no different from his ability to still an angry storm. All of these crises were manifestations of the threat of evil. And each of Jesus' responses was a sign of God's healing power that could rescue someone lost in the despair of a terminal illness as easily as he could pluck a foundering ship from the sea.

These distinctions made by biblical scholars should not be dismissed as irreverent assaults on the Gospels. The distinctions, in fact, represent a responsible attempt to understand the nature of the Gospel material. It is one thing to say that all of the Gospel miracles have the same basic significance (i.e., signs of God's redeeming power in Jesus); it is quite another thing to say that all of them are to be considered narrations of historical fact with no further refinement. Our purpose is not to develop a full-blown apologetic regarding the miracle stories, but some discussion of the nature miracles helps clarify our more central task of discovering what this Gospel material tells us about Jesus.

We discussed in the opening chapter how the basic traditions about Jesus were transmitted and shaped in the life of the church. There is no question that the church's faith in Jesus as the Risen Lord, as the fulfillment of God's promise to Israel, has left its imprint on the Gospel account of his life. This does not falsify the Gospel story but gives it an aura of interpretation that was possible only after the community had experienced resurrection faith. Only then were his followers able to comprehend the full significance of Jesus' life and teaching. The fruits of this fuller understanding are presented to us in the church's Gospels.

We should keep this in mind when we consider the question of the nature miracles. We should be aware, for instance, that the ability to control nature by calming the winds or by walking across the waves is an attribute of Yahweh himself in the Old Testament Scriptures. Psalm

65, for example, hymns the power of Yahweh who "stills the roaring of the seas, the roaring of their waves and the tumult of the peoples." In Psalm 89, the mighty Lord is the one who "rules over the surging of the sea," who "stills the swelling of its waves." The book of Job speaks of Yahweh who "treads upon the crests of the sea" (9:8).

We should be aware too that such miracles as the multiplication of the loaves and even the raising of the dead have Old Testament prefigurements. The prophet Elisha fed a hundred men with 20 barley loaves, and there was such bounty that some was left over (2 Kings 4:42-44). The heavenly manna of the Exodus story illustrates God's care for his people through the miraculous multiplication of seemingly insufficient rations. The great prophet Elijah brings back the son of the widow of Zarephath from the dead. Elisha does the same for the Shunammite's son.

And, finally, we must acknowledge that the Christians' own experience of the power of the spirit of the Risen Lord present in the church touches their reflection on the life of Jesus. Jesus' gestures in the multiplication story echo the ritual of the Eucharist (Mark 6:41). The disciples' plea for help in Matthew's version of the stilling of the storm uses the words of a Christian ejaculation, "Lord, save us!" (8:25). The raising of Lazarus prefigures the resurrection of Jesus himself. Peter's ability to walk on the waves like his Master and his failure to sustain the power of his faith symbolize the plight of the ordinary Christian in moments of crisis.

To acknowledge the rich complexity of these Gospel accounts does not mean that we explain away the nature miracles. But it does suggest caution in asserting that all of the Gospel miracle stories should be read as literal descriptions of events as they happened. At the root of these traditions may well have been some extraordinary display of Jesus' healing and calming power in a moment of crisis. Christian prayer and Christian faith have infused the accounts with rich imagery drawn from the Hebrew Scriptures and their own church experience. In some particular instances, the passage of Gospel tradition through the experience of the church may have had more than incidental effect on the final form of the story. Jesus' cursing of the fig tree is a miracle story that is notoriously unique. It seems arbitrary on Jesus' part—it was not even the season for figs—and incongruous with the purposeful use of his power in the rest of the Gospel story. It originally may have been a *parable* of Jesus about a fig tree rather than a miracle story. In Luke's Gospel, that is what we have (cf. Luke 13:6-9). The discovery of the shekel coin in the mouth of the fish also seems a bit fanciful. It suggests that this wondrous detail was not an original part of the story. Examples like these smack of the art of storytelling, the kind of affectionate embellishment that easily could have crept into the tradition as Christian preachers and catechists recounted the deeds of the Master.

But our discussion of the influence of the church's faith on the form of the nature miracles should not distract us from the fundamental statement they assert about Jesus. At this point, the message of the nature miracles is little different from that of the other types of miracles, even though the nature miracles may bear more evident traces of faith illumination. All of these acts signify that the healing and redeeming power of God was experienced by those to whom Jesus ministered. Later Christians would be able to understand more fully the implications of that power in Jesus. But the Gospel tradition leaves little doubt that Jesus' own contemporaries considered him a man of extraordinary force and power, a power that could liberate and heal, a power that could come only from God.

Miracles and Faith

Our description of Jesus as a powerful miracle worker could easily lead us astray. If we are tempted to think of him as a first-century Captain Marvel, then we have wandered far from the Gospel. One of the distinctive traits of the Gospel portrait is that Jesus, instead of being a ready dispenser of divine cures, was in fact a *reluctant* miracle worker. Precisely here, in the soberness of the Gospel portrayal, do we begin to discover those unique and fresh characteristics that stamp the authenticity of the Gospel tradition.

The Gospels seldom, if ever, portray Jesus as taking the initiative in using his healing powers. He does not roam around curing everyone in sight. The sick and the poor come to *him*. An occasional, critical need that he happens upon, such as the funeral procession of the widow's son, will draw from Jesus an immediate response. But in almost all cases, Jesus must be asked by those who seek to be cured.

The Gospels seem to indicate that Jesus' healing power sometimes overwhelmed him, perhaps even made him wish he did not have such extraordinary drawing power. After his first day of ministry in Capernaum, he slips away to a lonely spot in the desert. His disciples are forced to "track him down" (Mark 1:35). As the pace of his ministry quickens and his fame spreads, he avoids the larger towns and tries to stay in the countryside. But still, the Gospel notes (Mark 1:45), "people kept coming to him from all sides." Even when he works a cure, Jesus seems to fear the commotion it inevitably causes. Over and over again, the Gospels note that Jesus tells those cured, such as the Galilean leper or Jairus and his wife, "not a word to anyone" (Mark 1:44).

What is the meaning of all this? Undoubtedly some of the Gospel writers' own theological purpose may be at work here. The reverential approach of the petitioners to Jesus may reflect the conviction of the evangelists and the tradition before them that such was the way the believer should approach his saving Lord. The frequent injunctions to silence following Jesus' cures also might be part of Mark's subtle way of indicating that Jesus' messianic identity could easily be misunderstood; it should be reflected on carefully before the believer applies traditional titles to the Risen Lord. But even when we responsibly honor the presence of such theological interpretation in the Gospels, we are still left with a surprising residue of material that suggests that Jesus was hardly carried away by the power he seemed to possess. He certainly did not want it to become the identifying mark of his mission.

Perhaps nothing in the Gospel tradition emphasizes this reluctance more than the way Jesus deals with those who come to him looking only for these spectacular "signs." In the synoptic Gospels, when Pharisees demand some great marvel capable of convincing them of Jesus' authenticity, he vigorously refuses: "With a sigh from the depths of his spirit he said, 'Why does this age seek a sign? I assure you, no such sign will be given it!' " (Mark 8:12). John's Gospel in particular picks up this note about Jesus. Jesus seems depressed that the royal official in Capernaum appears interested only in Jesus' healing power: "Unless you people see signs and wonders, you do not believe" (John 4:48). A suspicion about those who seek only for "signs" characterizes the Johannine Jesus. The easily bought allegiance of the crowds that had witnessed his powers did not delude Jesus. "Jesus would not trust himself to them because he knew them all. He needed no one to give him testimony about human nature. He was well aware of what was in man's heart" (John 2:24-25).

At the climax of John's Gospel, Jesus exclaims: "Blessed are those who have not seen yet believe" (20:29). This statement provides the key to Jesus' reluctance. If anything characterizes the Gospel miracle tradition and sets it off from any analogies in Greek or Jewish literature, it is the consistent link between miracles and faith. What Jesus demands of those who come to him, either to learn or to be cured, is that they should totally trust him and his message. They were expected to believe in him, in the sense that they would acknowledge that what Jesus said and did was the work of God. If people were not willing to accept

Jesus on his own terms, if they came to him merely to exploit his power without appreciating his mission, then in Jesus' eyes they would be indulging in a magic game that had nothing to do with the purpose of his life.

Examples of this link between miracle and faith crowd the Gospels. The leper is cleansed because he approaches Jesus with a firm expression of faith: "If you will to do so, you can cure me" (Mark 1:40). The faith of the paralytic's friends assures his forgiveness and cure (Mark 2:5). Jesus tells the woman with the hemorrhage, "It is your faith that has cured you" (Mark 5:34). It is faith too that restores Bartimaeus' sight on the outskirts of Jericho (Mark 10:52). Jesus' amazement at the faith of the gentile centurion and the Canaanite woman triggers his response to their needs.

Conversely, lack of faith or mere curiosity about Jesus' healing power stands in the way of Jesus' miracles. A surprisingly blunt text of Mark notes that Jesus "could not" work miracles in his home town of Nazareth "so much did their lack of faith distress him" (6:5). In the parallel text of Matthew, this notice is changed to read: "he did not" work miracles there. But Mark's rendition retains the straightforward character of the original. The inability of Jesus to work miracles when faith in him was not present is no different from his refusal to grant the Pharisees' request for some spectacular sign or his overall diffidence about being labeled a miracle worker. What Jesus wanted was that people should believe in him, should recognize in him the power and compassion of his Father. Jesus never used miracles to bludgeon people into belief. They would have to take him on his own terms. Could they recognize in him, in his parables, his words of wisdom, his critique of the law and of legalism, in his compassion for the poor and the outcasts the authenticity of Jesus' message, the fact that Jesus was the Son who revealed his Father? If they could not or would not, then Jesus would never work a miracle to force faith. It had to be a genuine response to him, or it was nothing.

But if there was faith, then the miracle had already begun: the miracle of a transformed life, of healed alienation, of liberated legalism, of compassion refound. The physical cures were simply dramatic illustrations of the fundamental restoration Jesus worked in everyone whom he touched and who believed in him. That is why "miracle," in the spectacular sense of the word, was decidedly second place in Jesus' ministry. And that is why those who sought only to test or to exploit Jesus' power, such as certain Pharisees or Herod Antipas, would never be acknowledged by Jesus. But those who came with faith, totally willing to accept Jesus and his mission, are healed, whether by the power of a physical cure or, in the case of the prostitute, by the power of his love. To all, Jesus' message is basically the same: "Your faith has been your salvation" (Luke 7:50).

Like other portions of the Gospel material, the miracle stories add another stroke to the portrait of Jesus. We can acknowledge readily that the community's post-Easter faith in Jesus as the Risen Lord has helped shaped the miracle tradition and has embellished details here and there—perhaps even some entire stories. We can recognize too that the individual evangelist adds further dimension to the miracles when it fits into the overall framework of his Gospel. But some aspects of the Gospel miracle stories range across all of the Gospels and throughout the various layers of the general Gospel tradition. It is precisely these characteristics that smack of the vigor and freshness of Jesus. Jesus and the testimony of his contemporaries stand at the root of the miracle tradition.

The miracles tell us a few more things about Jesus. They tell us that his contemporaries experienced him as a man of uncommon power, a charismatic man who had the awesome power to heal, to bring calm to crisis, to call forth the very best in the people who trusted him. The miracle stories tell us too that Jesus was a man of absolute integrity. His healing power never stepped outside the bounds of his own life mission, never betrayed the purpose of his ministry. He preached a God of love and compassion, and his care for the poor and his response to their pain translated his words into action. He preached a call to service and human freedom; therefore he never exploited his power or used it for his own grandeur. He claimed that his "meat" was to do the will of his Father. Thus anyone who came to Jesus wishing to toy with his supposed magic but unwilling to be caught up in the Father's work would never receive a sign from Jesus.

We find in the miracle stories, as in other parts of the Gospel heritage, that steady testimony to the absolute wholeness and utter genuineness of Jesus of Nazareth. He was a man so close to his God that God's own creative power flowed out from him in healing waves. He was a man so dedicated to God's work that his own fascinating power seemed to embarrass him; at times it seemed to get in the way of his message. But, most of all, Jesus was a man so charged with God's own compassion and love that any cry of pain or confusion drew from him an instant response of healing and restoration.

Chapter 6

Death and Victory

Why would a person like Jesus be put to death? The Gospels portray him as a man of absolute integrity, humane and compassionate, a healer and a reconciler, a man at ease with the poor and the outcasts. But the Gospels also affirm unanimously that Jesus was executed as a criminal, practically abandoned, without the comfort of his friends or the satisfaction of a completed mission. How did this happen? And what do the Gospels tell us about Jesus as he faced death? No Gospel portrait would be complete without the Passion.

If we take the Gospels at face value, it would seem that facing death meant something quite different to Jesus than it would to us. For most of us, death is a cold and bewildering horror lurking at an unknown crossroad of life. We know nothing about it. Most of the time, we would prefer not even to think about it. Was Jesus' attitude toward death anything like this? At first glance, we might be tempted to say no. The Gospels have Jesus predict his death in startling detail several times during his ministry. He seems to speak of death with a splendid calm, accurately predicting the desertion of his friends and the betrayal by his enemies. When the moment of his Passion arrives, Jesus seems almost to host the event—lecturing his captors, assuring the release of his disciples, befuddling his inquisitors with a mixture of brilliant replies and majestic silence. There is suffering and humiliation involved, of course; but Jesus seems to ride above it all, certain of his ultimate triumph.

But if the experience of death was really like this for Jesus, would he be genuinely human? If his death were something that he ran toward all his life—placidly, knowingly, confidently—could we say, as our faith insists we must, that Jesus was thoroughly a man, sharing everything human but our alienation from God? At the very least, we would have to say that Jesus' view of death was quite different from the experience of most human beings.

We know, however, that the discord between the Christian contention that Jesus was truly human—as well as truly divine—and the Gospel suggestion that he faced death in a superhuman way can be muted by sorting the Gospel perspective from our own. As we have emphasized repeatedly, the Gospels view Jesus in light of resurrection faith. They do not attempt a psychological profile of Jesus. They do not chart his development, his attitudes, his inner thoughts and conflicts. Rather, the Gospels, like all Christian theology, proclaim Jesus as Risen Lord, as the fulfillment of God's promise, as the supreme moment of creation and history where the very life of God is revealed. All incidents recorded about his life are seen in this light; every word attributed to him has been etched by this faith.

Thus when we ask how Jesus as man viewed his death and what were the factors that led up to it, we are asking questions that are not the same questions the Gospel accounts seek to answer. For them, the life and death of Jesus are to be read "backwards"—that is, as prelude to his resurrection. The Gospel question becomes: How did all of these events fit into God's plan of salvation? Old Testament prophecy and the faith experience of the Christians themselves are used to show how Jesus' life and ministry ultimately were destined to move from death to glory. Acknowledging the resurrection perspective of the Gospels does not mean that we have to abandon our legitimate question about Jesus' human view of death. It only means that we must pick our way carefully through the Gospel material to discover once more something about the man behind the traditions.

Perhaps the most revealing Gospel passage for helping us track down Jesus' own attitude toward death is the Gethsemane scene. There, the mantle of resurrection faith seems to fall back. For a brief moment, we have a glimpse of Jesus struggling with death, as every human must. He is terrified. He pleads that the "hour," the "cup" of his suffering might pass. He reaches out to his friends for support as the terrible finality of death bears down on him. Here is death as it must have appeared to Jesus—not as a masquerade, not as a moment when divine knowledge could defuse death of its threat, but as a moment of genuine darkness and fright. He had been convinced that his mission was right. He had experienced God as his Father. He had believed that the Father had called him to his work for the Kingdom. Jesus had felt the power of his own preaching and had seen the healing effect of his touch. He had gathered disciples, and he had hoped to share with them the urgency of his mission. But now it all seemed to be slipping away. His ministry had not drawn the response he longed for. The crowds have not been converted. His worst fears about their superficial allegiance had been realized. The religious leadership had become his enemies. His own disciples were numbed by terror and confusion, about to abandon him to save themselves. Death seemed the only certainty.

What brought Jesus to this moment? How in the face of so much threat and failure was he able to say his prayer of trust: "Not my will, Father, but yours be done"? How could he have stood up from his prayer and turned to face his captors with enough trust left to believe still that his mission was not defeated? The tragic death of Jesus of Nazareth demands that we search the Gospel story for the answers.

The Opposition

Jesus' death does not break into the Gospel story unexpectedly. Almost from the beginning, the rumble of opposition and hostile threats against his life are heard in the background. The source of opposition is not some faceless and senseless plot against Jesus. Nor is it the result of a fated divine drama. It is Jesus' own determined actions that provoke the opposition to him and gradually make his enemies determined enough to kill him. In our study of Jesus' words and deeds, we have alluded to the opposition he caused, but it might be worthwhile to summarize it here.

First, throughout the Gospel accounts, practically from the very beginning of his ministry, Jesus draws fire because of his association with sinners and outcasts. Jesus' message was one of compassion and love, a love that extended to the clean and the unclean, to sinners as well as the righteous. He refused to be hemmed in by the smug taboos that human tradition had built around those who were unable or unwilling to keep the Law. He preached to these outcasts, he healed them, he offered them hospitality, and he loved to be with them.

Reaction was quick and vicious. Jesus' ministry became unpalatable to the religious leadership of his day; it tore holes in their very conception of what religion was. The Pharisees, for example, had limited the traditional term of God's beloved "poor" to those who kept the Law. But Jesus insisted that it was the genuinely poor, the materially poor, who were God's favorites and the prime beneficiaries of his Kingdom. The religious leaders had declared the "unclean" and sinners to be unworthy of God's grace. But Jesus said they especially were destined to receive it. Jewish society considered women as little more than slaves. But Jesus ignored their strictures, and he made several women his most trusted followers.

Thus Jesus' basic conviction that Yahweh was a God of love, the *Abba* whose love was offered to all—the just and the unjust, good and bad, poor and not poor—was not a harmless, pious sentiment. It was the basic insight of a mission that became an affront to the piety of his day. It transformed the very notion of religion. And Jesus would have to pay a price for his conviction. The murmuring and the offense that Jesus so frequently provoked by his ministry soon hardened into steely hatred.

But that was not the only root cause of Jesus' death. As we saw, some of the sharpest conflicts between Jesus and his opponents were over questions of the Jewish Law. Good sense and a respect for the documents we have available should warn us against typecasting Jesus and his opponents. The Jewish leaders were not mindless legalists, completely oblivious to love of God and love of neighbor—the very goals toward which the prescriptions of the Law were directed. Nor was Jesus an iconoclast, bent on destroying every attempt at order and regulated observance. There are too many sayings of Jesus that encourage respect for the Law, and too many instances from his own life that show him observing the Law, for us to build Jesus into a religious anarchist. And we have noted too that some of the bitter edge that marks Jesus' words was shaped by later controversies between Pharisaic Judaism and the young Christian church.

Jesus' critique of the Law and the opposition he provoked spring from a subtler base. Jesus recoiled from the delicate smugness that a concern with religious law easily can breed. The heart of genuine religion was the intimate bond of love between the Father and his children. True fidelity could be nothing less than a full, loving response to that gift of love. This is the center that judges all else, prescriptions of the Law included. Being religious can never be measured by the number of laws kept. Its only qualitative test is whether our own response to the needs of others matches the unselfish quality of God's love for us. Thus if the Sabbath regulations stood in the way of responding to need, Jesus did not hesitate to set them aside. If piety and tradition became so encrusted with formalism that they hampered genuine love, then their shallowness should be unmasked. If acts of mercy or of asceticism became podiums for one's sense of righteousness, then they were to be declared a sham.

So it was Jesus' own integrity and compelling honesty that led him to face-offs with his opponents on questions of Law. He was affronting their own self-image as the "saved," daring to teach the teachers of religion what faith in Yahweh really meant. It was a lesson his contemporaries could not bear, and as the Gospel ominously notes, "They began to plot . . . how they might destroy him" (Mark 3:6).

Another note of opposition registered in the Gospels is perhaps subtler than the ones we have listed above. The Gospels call it Jesus' "authority." The title most commonly applied to him in the Gospels is "teacher." But the Gospels also insist that Jesus did not teach as the scribes and Pharisees. For them, to teach "with authority" meant to cite suitable traditions, to appeal to the opinions of former rabbis. But never in any of Jesus' sayings does he cite another rabbi; never does he appeal to the weight of another's opinion. Even his citation of Scripture serves only to confirm what he himself already had stated confidently. The source of Jesus' authority is his own experience. From his intimate life of prayer with his Father and from a prayerful searching of the Scriptures, Jesus had forged the basic convictions that animated his life and ministry. Basic convictions about God as a loving Father and about love as fundamental bond of human relationships were joined to an unshakable integrity that translated principle into action. Jesus' words and actions took on an authority that affronted his critics and drew forth their cries of blasphemy.

He dared to address God in such affectionate terms that a properly pious Jew would be shocked. His own public prayers that he shared with his disciples were direct and uncluttered, so different from the overly deferential and verbally burdened prayers of many of his contemporaries. He tendered his own conclusions about what was proper on the Sabbath; he had unorthodox views about the regulations for ritual purity. And he was not afraid to make his views known with an air of quiet confidence that so often reduced his opponents to rage.

The things he did reflected that same determined conviction. He sought out the poor and the outcasts because he was sure they needed him. He was diffident about the commotion his miracles caused; but when the sick approached him, his healing touch was unhesitant. The voice that commanded the evil spirits to leave their victims brimmed with power. And he was not afraid to lead that ragtag group of baffled disciples and tattered onlookers into his opponents' own nests. He dined with Pharisees, unshaken by the critical stares that tested everything he did. Even the affectionate gratitude of a prostitute did not embarrass him when he dined with Simon the Pharisee. He commended her, and he exposed the hypocrisy of his host. He led a large parade of exuberant followers into Jerusalem, the capital city, on the eve of the great feast of Passover. He must have known that such a popular display would distress the Jewish authorities and rattle the nerves of the Romans. But he was convinced that his mission was right; and at least for this one time, when he knew that the final crisis was almost upon him, he was not afraid to let the power of his mission intimidate those who opposed him. The same triumphant surge would carry him into the Temple itself: He, a Galilean peasant who should have been blinking in awe, instead cleared commercialism from the Temple courtyard. Like one of the prophets of the past, Jesus chose a dramatic gesture to let his countrymen know that the repentance and reform he had preached in the countryside of Galilee applied with equal rigor to the center of power and worship in Jerusalem.

This determined sense of mission, never fanatical, never demagogic, characterized Jesus' every action. It gave him the forceful sense of authority that provoked a continuing chorus of exclamation in the Gospels: "What does this mean? A completely new teaching in a spirit of authority!" (Mark 1:27). "They were awestruck; all gave praise to God, saying, 'We have never seen anything like this!' " (Mark 2:12). Such authority could be viewed only as a threat to the religious and political establishment of Israel. And the threat became so unnerving that it eventually would bring about a most unlikely alliance of Jew and Roman to cope with it.

Reading the Signs

In chapter 16 of Matthew's Gospel, we are told that Jesus chided his opponents' lack of discernment in these words: "In the evening you say, 'Red sky at night, the day will be bright'; but in the morning, 'Sky red and gloomy, the day will be stormy.' If you know how to interpret the look of the sky, can you not read the signs of the times?" (16:2-3). Many scholars doubt that these words were originally in the Gospel; they are absent in many of the oldest and best manuscripts. Be that as it may, the words still ring with the solid good sense that characterizes so many of Jesus' sayings. And if his opponents were blind to the significance of Jesus' actions, he was not blind to theirs. The Gospels tell us in a variety of ways that Jesus predicted his tragic death. The source of that prediction did not have to be confined to some sort of supernatural vision of the fateful hour of Passion. Jesus could know by doing what he exhorted the Jewish leaders to do: reading the signs of the times.

First, he could hardly be unaware of the hostility of the religious leaders. The Gospel story is marked with constant conflict. And Jesus must have realized the ominous significance of the fact that groups such as the Sadducees and the Pharisees, normally at odds with each other, were united in opposition to him. But the Gospels also make clear that Jesus' differences with these groups and others prominent in the Judaism of his time were not on a factional basis. He did not differ with the Pharisees because they were Pharisees or the Zealots because they were Zealots. The positions he took on individual questions were not on some party basis; they were due to his own deepest convictions and unbending integrity. As a result, we can surmise that Jesus found himself out of step with almost every major party prominent in his day.

He sided with the Pharisees in upholding the legitimacy of oral interpretation of the Law and the responsible integration into the mainstream of Jewish thought of new ideas such as the resurrection of the body (cf. Mark 12:18-27). Thus he offended the conservative Sadducees, the Temple-based group that considered such liberalism unorthodox. But, as we have seen repeatedly, Jesus' natural kinship with the Pharisaic movement was aborted when he critiqued the excesses of their legalism. The Gospels say almost nothing about the Zealots, but we know that these political activists were a growing force in Jesus' day. We can surmise that their hopes of a popular uprising against Roman occupation might have caused initial interest in this Galilean rabbi who had such rapport with the peasants and who fearlessly preached that the moment of the Kingdom was now. Perhaps this was the promised leader, the Messiah, who could galvanize the people's resistance and restore Israel to the glory of the Maccabean independence. The Zealots, however, firmly believed that violence was an acceptable means for bringing about God's Kingdom. But Jesus was a pacifist. He went so far as to suggest to his followers that they "offer no resistance to injury" (Matthew 5:39). If a Roman soldier should impound horse or donkey to carry him for a mile, then the disciples should be willing to offer an extra mile (Matthew 5:41). And anyone who took up the sword in the cause of the Kingdom, Jesus warned, would be promoting destruction not liberation (Matthew 26:52). These were hardly the words of a revolutionary, at least not the kind the Zealots preferred. Even worse, Jesus was declaring that the Kingdom was open to sinners, to those who were outside the Law. He even seemed to hint that the Kingdom would welcome the gentile. For the Zealots, this was nothing less than heresy. The glory of Israel was reserved only for those Jews who observed the Law strictly; anyone else, whether Jew or gentile, was destined for destruction. Thus the Zealots would have been disillusioned by Jesus; they could be expected to have nothing but contempt for the way he squandered his power.

There were other groups at the time of Jesus, some we know very little about. The Gospels do not mention the Essenes, although they were an influential movement of Jesus' day. We do not know if Jesus ever dealt with the Essenes. But even among them he would have found little support. They may have shared his criticism of the hypocrisy that had crept into the piety of their day. Both the Essenes and Jesus felt that the Temple needed reform. But the Essenes certainly would not have approved of Jesus' lifestyle. Their rigorous asceticism would not be comfortable with this "wine bibber and glutton" (Matthew 11:19). Nor were they likely to understand how this Galilean peasant could claim to be doing God's work when he was to be found at the supper table of rich and poor alike. And he seemed to be constantly in the questionable company of tax collectors, sinners, and prostitutes. In reaction to these corruptive influences, the Essenes had sought a monastic form of life. Jesus would not have found allies here.

The Gospels, then, indicate that Jesus was something of a lonely figure—though not in the sense that he did not enjoy people or was anti-social. The picture is far from that. Rather, no one seemed to understand or accept his vision of life. He had no firm friends or followers who shared knowingly and enthusiastically in the great mission he felt swept up in. The crowds were impressed, but they really had not caught the seriousness of what he was telling them. The disciples had left everything to follow him; but he could not be sure that they really understood what he had taught them, and he often found their excitement about him and his cause laced with ambition for themselves.

On some of those lonely retreats into prayer and reflection that the Gospels tell us Jesus regularly took, he must have agonized over his isolation. Certainly he had not planned or hoped that it would turn out this way. He must have wished that his message would have thrilled the Pharisees and the priests just as much, if not more, than it would the poor and the sinners. But it had not worked. Not only had the leaders failed to be impressed, but they considered him a threat—so much of a threat that they were consulting together on how to get rid of him. No group seemed to be lining up on his side. There was not much he could do. He could not change his message without destroying himself. Yet if he did not change, his opponents were determined to destroy him. Jesus could read the signs of the times.

But the ugly mood of his opponents was not the only sign that Jesus had to read as he faced up to the possibility of his death. He knew his Scriptures, and he knew the traditions of his people. There were signs there as well that could help him understand the crisis that loomed before him.

The Prophet

Jesus' generation was bothered by the absence of prophets among the people. No great prophets had risen up in Israel since the time of Malachi, almost five centuries before Jesus. The succession of prophetic voices that for centuries had graced the pages of Jewish history and had assured the people of the presence of God's Spirit among them had been broken off. The rabbis fretted about this prophetic void. Was it a sign of divine anger? Were they being punished for the many times they had rejected the prophets and even abused them? Or was this disturbing silence itself a sign that the final age was about to break upon the world, the time when God's liberating Spirit once more would flood Israel with its redeeming light?

Rabbinic speculation about the "quenching of the spirit" was matched by a popular piety that attempted to do honor to the prophets, particularly to those who had been rejected and murdered by Israel. Monumental tombs were built in the large cemetery that covered the Kidron valley, the deep ravine separating the Temple from the Mount of Olives. Public prayers honored the martyred prophets and expressed Israel's repentance for the sins of its ancestors.

This popular cult helped Jesus understand his own plight. The Gospels indicate that the traditional image in which Jesus conceived his own call and service was that of a prophet. Like the prophets of old, Jesus was convinced that God's Spirit had called him. The force and instinct guiding his ministry was the Spirit. Over and over in the Gospels, Jesus' possession of the Spirit is affirmed. The Spirit decends upon him at the inaugural vision of his baptism (Mark 1:10). The Spirit propels him into his dramatic confrontation with evil (Mark 1:12). By the power of the Spirit he casts out demons (Matthew 12:28). The people who come in contact with Jesus also understand him as a prophet, as the Gospels repeatedly confirm: "He is a prophet equal to any of the prophets" (Mark 6:15); "A great prophet has risen among us" (Luke 7:16). His role as prophet is mocked by the soldiers at his trial (Mark 14:65).

Jesus does not reject this popular estimate of him as prophet; there are explicit sayings where he himself adopts it. Both Luke and Matthew attest that Jesus applied to himself the great prophetic manifesto of Isaiah 61. In

Luke's account, Jesus begins his ministry by citing the opening words of chapter 61 of Isaiah: "The Spirit of the Lord is upon me; therefore, he has anointed me . . ." (4:18). And in Matthew 11:5 (cf. also Luke 7:22), Jesus quotes again from Isaiah 61 to satisfy the messengers sent from John the Baptist: "Go back and report to John what you hear and see: the blind recover their sight, cripples walk, lepers are cured, the deaf hear, dead men are raised to life, and the poor have the good news preached to them."

Jesus, however, did not consider himself simply one more prophetic voice that had been sent to Israel. He was convinced that the final age was about to dawn, that God was drawing near to man to establish his Kingdom. Therefore Jesus' prophetic message was not a voice in chorus but the finale. He was the last of the prophets. And the greatest.

It was this consciousness that gave such force and authority to Jesus' ministry, and it was his self-image as prophet that helped Jesus understand the inevitability of his death. Just as Israel had rejected the prophets before him, so he too would suffer rejection. Two sayings of Jesus in the Gospel seem to spring from this consciousness and thus give us an insight into Jesus' own understanding. The first occurs in chapter 23 of Matthew (with a parallel passage in Luke 11:47ff.). The entire chapter is a bitter indictment of the Jewish leaders. This section undoubtedly took on some of the harsh tones of later debate between church and synagogue. But these particular verses, attested in both Gospels, are rooted in the situation of Jesus' own day: "Woe to you scribes and Pharisees, you frauds! You say, 'Had we lived in our forefathers' time we would not have joined them in shedding the prophets' blood.' Thus you show that you are the sons of the prophets' murderers. Now it is your turn: fill up the vessel measured out by your forefathers." Jesus sees his own fate as a share in the cruel destiny of the rejected prophets. As his people had done in the past, so now they would do to him.

The parable of the Tenants that occurs in all three synoptic Gospels was used by the early church to situate Jesus' fate in the broad spectrum of salvation history. Several of the original details have been allegorized in Christian preaching to bring it in line with the events of history. But the story as told by Jesus was a pointed symbol of his fate as a prophet. The owner of a vineyard—a traditional Jewish symbol for Israel itself—sends out a series of messengers to collect the fruits of the harvest from his tenants. The workers resent the intrusion of the absentee landlord; they mistreat and even kill the envoys he sends. "Last of all," the story notes, he sent his son, certain the workers would not dare reject him. But the laborers blindly kill the son as well, hoping thereby to be able to take over the vineyard. Their treachery insures their own doom.

The point of the parable was not lost on Jesus' audience. He places himself in the line of the prophets, the long chain of messengers ignored and mistreated by Israel. He himself is such a prophet—not merely a link in the chain, but the final and most important messenger, the King's own son. To reject him is to reject God's final word to Israel. At the conclusion of the parable, the Gospel ominously notes: "They (the Temple authorities to whom Jesus had addressed the story) wanted to arrest him at this, yet they had reason to fear the crowd. They knew well enough that he meant the parable for them" (Mark 12:12). By understanding himself as a prophet, Jesus gained not only a better grasp of his own ministry but a preview of his fate.

The Suffering Servant

There were other currents of thought in the heritage of Israel that could help Jesus read the signs of the times. One was the image of the Suffering Servant who gives his life to atone for the sins of Israel. The beautiful Servant

Song of Isaiah 53 is the most well-known expression of this image. The Servant, a mysterious figure who somehow represents all of the people of Israel, takes upon himself the sins of the people and by patient suffering atones for their guilt:

Yet it was our infirmities that he bore, our sufferings that he endured, While we thought of him as stricken, as one smitten by God and afflicted. But he was pierced for our offenses, crushed for our sins; Upon him was the chastisement that makes us whole, by his stripes we were healed (Isaiah 53:4-5).

We know that the early church turned often to this text in order to understand the meaning of Jesus' death and resurrection. But many scholars are hesitant to say whether Jesus himself used this image to interpret his own sufferings. The references to the Servant passages of Isaiah are relatively sparse in the Gospels, and some of the references that occur do not emphasize the idea of atonement as later church reflection would. There are some important reasons, however, for affirming that Jesus did draw upon this traditional image to understand his own destiny.

First, the idea of atoning suffering was a current of thought popular at the time of Jesus. The fact that so many innocent people had died heroic deaths during the Maccabean war of independence and during the often cruel occupation of the Romans had stirred speculation about the meaning of innocent suffering. As we noted, Judaism was not convinced that every incident of suffering and death could be traced to some personal sin. The truly innocent suffered as much as the guilty. Could it be that the death of an innocent man somehow atoned for the sins of others? Was it possible that the noble sufferings of one person somehow could heal the afflictions of others? Pure logic might consider the suggestion absurd, but human experience concluded otherwise. It was an experience of atonement in the midst of absurd suffering that inspired Isaiah's hymns, and it was a series of similar experiences that kept the idea alive in Jesus' own day.

And there are a couple of Gospel texts that suggest that Jesus and not just later church reflection applied the image of the atoning servant to himself. The first occurs in Mark's Gospel during the long journey from Galilee to Jerusalem. The disciples repeatedly resist Jesus' attempts to warn them of the fate that awaits him in Jerusalem. Finally, when the sons of Zebedee, James and John, blithely ask about positions of power in the Kingdom, Jesus calls all of his followers together to try once more to impress upon them the seriousness of the situation. The ambition and greed of the disciples show that they have not grasped the true meaning of Jesus' mission. They are merely aping the power plays of the Romans. Jesus continues: "It cannot be like that with you. Anyone among you who aspires to greatness must serve the rest; whoever wants to rank first among you must serve the needs of all. The Son of Man has not come to be served but to serve—to give his life in ransom for the many" (Mark 10:43-45).

The concluding phrase, which speaks of Jesus' death as a "ransom for the many," seems to echo the Hebrew text of Isaiah 53:10 that designated the Servant's death as "an offering for sin." Jesus consistently refused to subvert the purpose of his mission. His call was to serve, not to be served. He would not compromise or seek political power, even if doing so could have saved his own life and earned the allegiance of his people. He would not turn back from his call, even if his own disciples found his determination absurd. It may well have been in a moment like this that Jesus would have seen the fate of the Suffering Servant as a harbinger of his own destiny.

Another important set of texts is found in the accounts of the Last Supper. Each of the evangelists, although in very different ways, presents Jesus speaking of his death in the vocabulary of atonement. His blood will be poured out "on behalf of many" (Mark), " for the forgiveness of sins" (Matthew), or simply "shed for you" (Luke). His body will be "given for you" (Luke) or given "for the life of the world" (John, where the words are found in the long discourse of chapter 6). The unique formulations of the various Gospels are evidence that the early church has brought much of its own theology and Eucharistic experience to bear on these texts, so it is difficult for us to isolate the original form of Jesus' words. But at the very least, the Gospel tradition suggests that Jesus had his approaching death very much on his mind as he sat down to supper for the last time with his disciples. He certainly could see that the crisis was near, that perhaps within the next few hours his enemies would make their move against him.

The Gospels record many meals enjoyed by Jesus and his followers. The guest list often included not only his disciples but also outcasts, sinners, tax collectors, and other unworthies (cf., for example, Luke 5:29-30; 7:34; 15:1-2; 19:7). These moments of peace and joy must have deepened the bond of friendship between Jesus and his followers. But this night would be the last. Thus what normally would have been a festive meal with his friends became choked with the deep sadness of a last goodbye. His disciples probably were unaware of the poignancy of that moment. Their relaxed mood must have seemed touchingly vulnerable to Jesus who knew so well the chaos that soon would engulf those awkward and lovable men. It was at this moment that Jesus stood up to do his duty as host, to say the blessing over the cup and the bread. And it was then that he must have startled his friends by saying that the cup and the bread were symbols of his own death, a death like that of the Servant whose sufferings touched all of God's people. By seeing himself as Servant as well as prophet, Jesus could find meaning in the death his enemies' hostility seemed to promise. Neither of these traditions was simply a harbinger of certain death. Each promised victory. The word of the prophet was really God's Word; it could never be stilled. The sufferings of the Servant were not in vain; they would atone for the sins of many.

The paradoxical linking of death and victory was a deep current of Jewish faith. It was, in fact, a corollary of the Jew's trust that Yahweh was faithful. The precise way in which suffering and death could lead to new life was an impenetrable mystery. But no believing Jew could be convinced that the God of Israel would abandon those who trusted in him.This hope thrusts through many of the most exalted expressions of biblical faith. Psalm 22, one of the most magnificent hymns of the Old Testament, is an agonizing cry of faith. It expresses confidence that, in the midst of doubt and intense suffering, Yahweh would hear the cry of a just man "and not turn his face away from him" (22:25). The book of Wisdom, a biblical writing composed only a short time before Jesus' own day, repeats the same basic hope. It counters the cynicism of Israel's enemies with the belief that "the souls of the just are in the hand of God and no torment shall touch them. They seemed, in the view of the foolish, to be dead; and their passing away was thought an affliction and their going forth from us, utter destruction. But they are in peace" (Wisdom 3:1-3). The great vision of Ezekiel, who sees the desert floor scattered with dead men's bones, expresses the same unshakable hope. The word of God has the power to sinew those bleached bones together, to wrap them in flesh, and to breathe new life into them. Once again, the people of Israel, who had been crushed by their enemies, would rise up and return in triumph to God's holy city (cf. Ezekiel 37).

This theme of the vindication of the suffering of just men was very much an affirmation of Jewish faith in Jesus' time. These same biblical texts were favorites of Jesus' contemporaries. They were applied to their heroes who had died martyrs' deaths, and they supported the faith of an oppressed people as they longed for freedom. The texts also were used by the early Christians to help them understand the meaning of Jesus' death. Matthew and Mark place the words of Psalm 22 on Jesus' dying lips. A citation from the second chapter of the book of Wisdom becomes the ironic words that the mockers on Calvary hurl at the cross (Matthew 27:43). Matthew draws on Ezekiel's vision of the dry bones to describe the cosmic results of Jesus' obedient death (cf. Matthew 27:53). It seems sure that the early Christians were only following the lead of their Master.

Thus the rich heritage of Judaism helped Jesus "read the signs of the times." An awareness of that heritage also helps us understand the prominent place of the so-called "Passion predictions" in the Gospel literature. The Gospel of Mark has set the pattern, followed closely by Matthew and Luke and to a lesser extent by John. Three times during his last journey to Jerusalem, Jesus solemnly predicts his approaching ordeal: "He began to teach them that the Son of Man had to suffer much, be rejected by the elders, the chief priests and the scribes, be put to death, and rise three days later" (Mark 8:31). A later prediction is even more detailed: "We are on our way up to Jerusalem, where the Son of Man will be handed over to the chief priests and the scribes. They will condemn him to death and hand him over to the Gentiles, who will mock him and spit at him, flog him, and finally kill him. But three days later he will rise" (Mark 10:33-34).

There is little doubt that these and other predictions in the Gospels have been influenced by the church's memory of how the Passion actually turned out. The details of later events have been read back into the predictions. But we have seen how the core assertion of these predictions was part of Jesus' consciousness before the Passion. He knew of his enemies' hostility, and he knew what a mission like his own entailed. But the predictions also speak of victory. They are not simply Passion predictions but also *resurrection* predictions. Here too the basic validity of such a prediction can be rooted in Jesus' own awareness prior to his death and resurrection. Perhaps as a human being he could not know the precise way in which God would vindicate the sacrifice of his life. But he trusted his Father, his *Abba*. And as formidable as death might appear, it could not quench the faith of the Son of God.

Jesus' awareness that suffering and death are inevitable brings a muted soberness to his teaching. The words of Jesus and the drama of his life display a sense of deliberateness. He fears death but is not dominated by fear. He loves life but does not grip it too closely to himself. Morbidity never taints Jesus' awareness of death; he is a man of hope.

The Passion Story

We return to the garden of Gethsemane. The Jesus who prays there is entirely consistent with the Jesus of the rest of the Gospel story. Jesus was a human being, a Jew, a young man who had sensed the power of his mission and had hoped he could accomplish what he had set out to do. But Jesus was no fool. He knew that his enemies were serious, and he was aware of the fate of men before him who had preached with the same sort of Spirit-filled authority that he had. Death seemed certain. Fear was there, but so was trust, an even deeper instinct. And the prayer wrung from his heart was the very prayer that had marked every decision of his life: "Abba, Father . . . your will be done."

The account of the final hours that follow this moment of prayer dominate the Gospel story. For all four evangelists, the Passion is the target their entire Gospel moves toward. The events of Jesus' sufferings and death are told in a detailed, narrative fashion unlike any other segment of his life story.

There are a number of reasons for this concentration on the Passion. The death and resurrection of Jesus was the heart of the Christian message; so it is hardly surprising that the Gospels, which capsulate the message in story form, should concentrate their attention on this part of Jesus' life. It is also quite clear that the fact and manner of Jesus' death were by far the most baffling facets of Christian tradition. That Jesus, God's beloved Son and the promised Messiah, should die a criminal's death needed some explanation, not only to skeptical Jewish and Roman audiences but for believers. It had to be shown that Jesus was innocent and that his death, no matter how inappropriate it might seem, was really part of God's plan of salvation. As the young Christian church began to run into persecution and rejection, and when some of its members began to fall away from the faith, the distressed believers would turn with renewed appreciation to reflect on how their Lord had suffered before he entered into his glory. They could find support in the fact that he too had known failure and opposition but had never despaired.

Thus the Passion narrative was important for the faith of the early church. Many scholars think that the Passion story was among the very first products of Christian literature. The setting that formed it very likely was the liturgy, perhaps in a service similar to our present-day Good Friday liturgy. When the early Christians gathered to commemorate the Lord's death and resurrection, there would have been a solemn recitation of the traditional story of those final hours of Jesus. There would be readings from the Old Testament, the singing of psalms, and moments of prayer and reflection. As time went on and the service became more formalized, the recitation of the Passion story would have been honed into a smoother style, and many of the psalms and prayers would have been integrated into the story.

A setting like this helps account for some of the unique features of the Passion narratives as they are incorporated into the Gospels. The four evangelists often go their own way in presenting the details of other incidents in the life of Jesus, yet they maintain a rather amazing uniformity in their presentation of the Passion. This suggests that the form of the Passion story was largely established before the evangelists began to compose the Gospels. Even more important, the Passion narrative's allusion to the Old Testament is much more subtle and diffuse than in any other part of the Gospels. There are relatively few explicit quotations from the Old Testament. But the details of the story have been bonded so closely together with allusions to the Old Testament, particularly the psalms and the prophets, that it is often difficult to tell where the story leaves off and the allusion begins. For example, in the crucifixion scene alone, we can find Old Testament allusions for the following details in Mark's account: the offer of wine (Psalm 69), the division of Jesus' garments (Psalm 22), the presence of two robbers (Isaiah 53), the gestures and words of the mockers (Psalm 22; Wisdom 2), the darkness (Amos 8), Jesus' final prayer (Psalm 22), the offer of vinegar to drink (Psalm 69), the loud cry of Jesus (Psalm 31), the tearing of the Temple veil (Exodus 26).

This does not mean, of course, that all of these details are mere fabrications put into the story because they harmonize with the Old Testament. But it does mean that in the Passion story, as in the rest of the Gospel, the evangelists and the tradition before them were not simply reporting events but presenting history in the perspective of faith. And the reader of the Gospel is expected to approach the story with the same attitude of faith and prayerful reflection.

But when we ask the question "What exactly happened?" the historical nucleus known to us can be told briefly. The central fact is that Jesus was executed by the Romans. About that there is no doubt. Crucifixion was the basest form of Roman criminal punishment, reserved for slaves and non-citizens. Therefore Jesus was tried by a Roman court and found guilty. And we can presume, as the Gospels themselves suggest, that the charge against Jesus was not religious but political. The Romans would hardly have become excited about any Jew's claims to be a "Son of God" or a Messiah. But they would be interested if those claims implied political power, as Jesus' enemies suggested they did. And if Jesus and his followers had caused unrest in the occupied capital city during the nervous atmosphere of one of the great Jewish feast days, then the Romans certainly would be on the alert. It was probably in this fashion that the power of Rome moved against Jesus. Jesus was executed as a political insurgent—a truly ironic ending when we recall Jesus' refusal to adopt the Zealot program.

Despite the fact that Jesus was executed under Roman law, the Gospel accounts do not really concentrate on the role of the Romans. They focus instead on the role of the Jews, and it is here that the question "What actually happened?" becomes more delicate. The Gospel story implies that the Jews themselves formally tried Jesus before handing him over to the Romans. But many historians doubt that a formal trial would have been likely in these circumstances. More probably, the Jewish leaders held an informal strategy session prior to making their case before the Roman court. Christian concentration on Jewish involvement in the death of Jesus stemmed, in part, from the hurt and perplexity caused by the fact that the Jewish people had not accepted the Gospel message. And later Christians surely would not want to overemphasize *Roman* involvement when the young church's relationship to the authorities of the state at best was tenuous.

These influences on the Gospel accounts of the death of Jesus should not be forgotten by Christians of today. One of the most tragic and shameful blots on Christian history has been the use of the Passion story as an excuse for anti-Semitism. The issues the Gospel writers—most of whom were Jewish—were dealing with were religious not racial. They were trying to digest the fact that Israel, God's chosen people, had rejected Jesus and the message of his disciples. How could this be reconciled with God's will?

was the question the Passion accounts ultimately struggle with. The Passion story was never meant to be a perpetual indictment of the Jewish people. In fact, Paul, the Apostle to the gentiles and one of the most severe critics of Judaism, was convinced that the final moment of God's plan would be the eventual inclusion of Israel in the community of faith. For, as he insists in his epistle to the Romans, "God's gifts and his call are irrevocable" (11:29).

Thus the ultimate message of the Passion story is not polemical or racial; it is religious. And here the dark tones of the Passion story blend into the brilliant colors of the rest of the Gospel portrait. The central figure of the account is not the vacillating Roman governor, nor the Jewish interrogators, nor the angry mobs; it is Jesus. Jesus dominates the fateful sequence of those cruel scenes. And through the overlay of reverence and apologetic that tradition has molded into the story, we still can sense his presence. The same humaneness, the same integrity, the same authority, the same purposeful obedience to his Father's will are there. The Jesus of the miracle stories, the Jesus who teaches with authority, is the same Jesus who suffers yet believes. One of the remarkable features of the Passion story, quite distinct from some of the Jewish martyr accounts from the same period, is that there is very little concentration on the *physical* sufferings of Jesus. The mockeries, the scourging, even the crucifixion itself, are related in surprising understatement. Jesus is not painted as a martyr whose cruel death insures admiration. He is not a stoic ideal of endurance against all odds. Jesus is presented as the faithful believer. He is the just man who calls out to his God in the midst of agony and defeat, a man who trusts that even death cannot nullify God's promise.

And that is why none of the Gospels ends with the Passion. The story of the Passion is one of trust in the midst of death; its outcome is resurrection. Resurrection frames the Gospel portrait of Jesus. The Gospel narratives are complex, and the differences between the presentations of individual evangelists are substantial. But the basic message of the Gospel resurrection accounts are absolutely uniform: The trust of Jesus in his Father was vindicated. The miracles of Jesus were not the work of Beelzebul. His indictment of legalism was not presumptuous. The simplicity of his prayer and the intimate affection he tendered towards his Father were not too bold. His insistence on service and his indictment of violence were not visionary. Above all, his conviction that the Kingdom was coming was not an illusion. All of this, everything that Jesus said and did, was vindicated by the resurrection. The Kingdom of God had come: in him. Vindication is the final chapter of the Gospel story, the final stroke in its portrait of Jesus.

Chapter 7

Jesus and His Church

The main lines of our Gospel portrait of Jesus have been drawn. In reviewing it, Catholics may have difficulty finding some of the ideas and structures that make up essential parts of their faith life. There has been little discussion, for example, about the sacraments, about the doctrine of the Trinity, about forms of church authority, and so on. The omission of such items is not an attempt to question their validity or worth or to suggest that they have nothing to do with Jesus. Their absence in the preceding pages is a sign that most of them belong in a consideration of the life of the church rather than in a study of the life of Jesus.

The two stages should not be confused. Where Jesus "left off," the church begins. Most of the things we Christians today call doctrine and church structure derive from the church's reflection on the life, death, and resurrection of Jesus. As we bring our study to a close, it might be worthwhile to trace the circuit that links the life of the church to the life of Jesus. These concluding remarks cannot do adequate justice to what is an enormous question, but a broad overview at least might be helpful.

The Church Begins

"The church begins where Jesus left off." What does the statement mean? It should be obvious first that the band of disciples who followed Jesus during his ministry hardly could be called a "church," understood as a well-formed community of believers. Although they were constantly with Jesus, the original disciples had great difficulty understanding his teaching or the significance of his ministry. Their loyalty to him was constantly in question. And when the crisis of Jesus' death fell on that fragile band, they disintegrated in fear and disillusion. The Gospel tradition reported all of this, although we can surmise that the early church would have preferred to say something more heroic about the disciples. But the picture is realistic because the history was too glaring to be idealized away.

The "church," understood as a community of believers who share a common vision and are fired by a singular mission, really did not come into existence until the resurrection. Only after the disciples became convinced through personal experience that Jesus was alive, that he was risen from the dead—only after they had received the fruits of Jesus' victory over death in the form of the Spirit—did they find their courage and their conviction. Only then did the group of men and women who huddled in fear in Jerusalem understand who Jesus was and what his life had meant. Only then did they feel justified in taking up again the mission they once had shared in.

To acknowledge a distinction between the time of Jesus and the time of the church is not to deny the continuity. We obviously are talking about the same people. The disciples who began to preach on Pentecost were the same frightened men who had fled from the garden, who had denied Jesus in the courtyard of the high priest. And they carried their memories with them. Their memories of what sort of person Jesus was and of the wonderful things he said and did must have compounded their shame during the interval of their desertion, just as it would fire their joy once reconciliation had taken place. And we are talking about the same Jesus. Because of Jesus, the disciples had abandoned their professions and their families to make him the focus of their lives. Now the same thing was happening again—but in a new and startling way. Once again, Jesus was prodding them to leave behind an old life of fear and alienation and to join together in a new life of community and purpose.

It is hard to judge to what extent and in what form the continuity between his own life and succeeding generations of disciples occurred to Jesus in his human consciousness. Certainly he had gathered disciples and given them a share in his own ministry. And there are a number of sayings in the Gospel in which Jesus projected that the work of the Kingdom was to be long and difficult. He predicted too that the same difficulties of misunderstanding and hostility that plagued his own ministry would be the lot of disciples who came after him. By his own words, Jesus the man "did not know the exact day or hour" (Mark 13:32) when the final victory of God's Kingdom would be accomplished. For Jesus, as for every human being, the future was somewhat vague and uncertain. But he knew that his mission would have to continue, even if the exact way in which later generations would go about it may not have crossed his mind.

The early church, when it looked back on the life of Jesus, was able to see the continuity between its own mission and that of Jesus. The evangelists and their churches saw in Jesus' commissioning of his disciples their own marching orders. The dullness of the disciples and their refusal to accept suffering were understood as somber warnings for the church. And the ability of Jesus to rescue his followers from the crisis of sea and storm became images of the church's best instinct as it cried out to its Risen Lord to save it in new crises of persecution and loss of faith.

'Beyond' Jesus

So there was continuity between the life of Jesus and the life of the church. But when we examine what the newly formed church began to preach, we soon discover that continuity does not necessarily mean "more of the same." One of the most obvious illustrations of this is what the church began to say about Jesus. The church did not simply repeat the message of Jesus about the coming of the Kingdom. It began to focus on Jesus himself. "The proclaimer became the proclaimed," as several theologians have put it. With the hindsight of resurrection faith, the early church began to understand things about Jesus that his original disciples could never have appreciated during his lifetime. To illustrate this process with the careful nuance it calls for would take us far beyond the scope of this book. But some quick examples can help.

One of the first products of this process of understanding and interpretation—a process, by the way, that began immediately after the resurrection and continues to this day in the teaching of the church—was the application of "titles" to Jesus. The early preachers and teachers of Christianity began to apply to Jesus traditional titles, most of them borrowed from Judaism, that helped them identify the significance of Jesus' life, death, and resurrection. He was called "Lord," "Christ," "Son of David," "Son of God," "Son of Man," and so on. Almost all of these have worked their way into the Gospels, which, we know, reflect the church's post-resurrection faith and insight as much as they do historical traditions dating from the lifetime of Jesus. Some of these titles probably never were addressed to Jesus by his original followers. And even some of those that may have been used took on new and richer meaning as the early Church's appreciation of Jesus deepened.

An example in the latter category would be the title "Lord," in the Greek, *Kyrios*. This term certainly had religious meaning for the Jews who translated the Hebrew Scriptures into Greek in the centuries immediately preceding Jesus. *Kyrios* or "Lord" was used to translate the name of God, *Yahweh*, in the Hebrew Scripture. But the title also had a common secular usage, devoid of any religious connotation. It was a normal term of respect applied to such people as slave owners by their slaves or to people in authority by their subjects, a usage similar to the connotation of the English word "sir."

When the disciples addressed Jesus with the Aramaic (the language they normally would use rather than Greek) equivalent for this title, they would have meant it with its *secular* connotation. The early followers of Jesus hardly could have conceived of him as *Kyrios* in the full religious sense. But after the resurrection, when the church's understanding of Jesus began to deepen, and as the Christians moved out into the Greek-speaking world where *Kyrios* also had profound religious as well as secular meaning, then the title was applied to Jesus to express their belief that he was invested with divine power and authority.

The title surely has this significance in the early Christian hymn that Paul cites in his epistle to the Philippians:

So that at Jesus' name every knee must bend in the heavens, on the earth, and under the earth, and every tongue proclaim to the glory of God the Father: Jesus Christ is Lord (Kyrios)!" (2:10-11).

There are numerous instances in the rest of Paul's epistles where he applies the title to Jesus in an equally significant way. Later New Testament writings, such as the Gospels and the Acts of the Apostles, also employ the title with the profound understanding that resurrection faith had given it. When the disciples cry out, "Lord, save us!" (Matthew 8:25) in the midst of the storm at sea, the words are an affirmation of the divine power of Jesus to save. When Thomas kneels in belief to confess: "My Lord and my God" (John 20:28), the words brim with the fullness of resurrection faith.

Other New Testament titles reflect the same sort of maturing process that transformed them from secular or only half-understood religious titles into vehicles of mature Christian confession. It seems likely, for example, that Jesus himself did not prefer to be addressed as the "Messiah" (or its Greek equivalent, *Christ*) because he feared that the nationalistic political overtones it conveyed to the Jews would distort a proper understanding of his mission. Thus in Mark's Gospel, when Peter addresses Jesus as the "Christ," the leader of the disciples is told to be silent, and Jesus immediately begins to instruct his followers about the role that suffering and death had to play in his mission (cf. Mark 8:27-33). But after the resurrection, the early church did not hesitate to apply this title to Jesus; in the light of faith, it now could understand the kind of Messiah Jesus was. The early missionaries needed this title when preaching to Jewish audiences in order to convey their conviction that Jesus was indeed the one who fulfilled God's promises to Israel, the great leader whose advent capped centuries of hope. Therefore, in the early sermons of Acts and throughout the New Testament, Jesus is referred to as the Christ, so much so that the title soon became almost a proper name for Jesus.

Not all of the titles applied to Jesus had the same success in the early church. Perhaps the most startling example is the important title "Son of Man." Of all the titles assigned to Jesus in the Gospels, most biblical scholars would agree that this rather mysterious title was the one Jesus himself probably preferred. "Son of Man" is a literal translation of the Aramaic expression *bar nasa*, which is really equivalent in Aramaic to "man." The title has an exceedingly complex literary and religious tradition behind it, and biblical scholars are deeply divided about what it precisely meant for Jesus and the early church. One of the most important roots of the title is its use in the book of Daniel, a very late Old Testament book. The "Son of Man" who appears in the visions of this book is a vaguely mysterious figure, apparently representing Israel itself, who shares in the final victory of God's Kingdom. Some scholars believe that Jesus preferred this title precisely because of its vagueness. It suggested his representative role as a spokesman for Israel, and it implied the certain victory of the Kingdom that his ministry would provoke, but without the baggage of nationalistic expectations that accompanied a title like "Messiah."

As a title, "Son of Man" had significance for the early Jewish disciples since it is employed frequently in the words of Jesus preserved in the Gospel tradition. But it is a theological title practically ignored by the rest of the New Testament writings! As the church became more at home in gentile surroundings, the use of "Son of Man" as an identifying label for Jesus apparently gave way to more readily understandable titles such as "Lord" or "Son of God."

The use of theological titles, then, was one way the early Christians were able to express their maturing faith in Jesus. The same process reached out into broader concepts of Jesus' life and mission. Paul, for example, does not concern himself with the story of Jesus' life; rather, he steps back from the canvas to consider the cosmic significance of Jesus' central act of dying and rising. It is the mystery of death and resurrection that Paul makes the all-consuming focus of his theology in his letters to his convert churches. The redemptive act of Jesus is seen as making him the "first-born son" of countless future generations, the power of his resurrection touching all who believe in him. Or Jesus is the "new Adam" who, by his obedient death, overcomes the power of sin unleashed by the old Adam. Or Jesus is the great liberator who, through the power of his resurrection, shares with Christians his dignity as a Son of God so that we are no longer bound to the life of servitude and fear that marked the old Law. Or the Risen Jesus is seen as the Lord of the universe, the pattern for all of creation, the prince who rules over all the hostile powers that previously crippled the world. All of these Pauline images—and there are many more—reveal the same interpretive process reflected in the early titles.

Paul, of course, was not the only New Testament writer to do this kind of interpretive work. Almost all of the other New Testament authors do it in their own way. The author of the letter to the Hebrews, for instance, speaks of the redemptive work of Jesus in terms of a great heavenly liturgy, with the Risen Lord serving as the high priest who offers an eternally acceptable sacrifice to God his Father. The imaginative author of the book of Revelation adapts the literary style of Jewish apocalyptic writing to show how the church will triumph with its Lord over the forces of evil and persecution. And we tried to show in our opening chapter that the Gospel writers themselves are involved in the very same process, portraying the profound significance of Jesus' life and death by their distinctive accounts of the Gospel story. This process could be called "theology"—that is, bringing the power of reason and culture to bear in a reverent understanding of faith. It is theology in this broad sense that the evangelists are engaged in. Mark expresses a theology when he emphasizes the Passion of Jesus in order to explain to his church how suffering is a part of the Christian picture. Matthew does the work of theology by emphasizing Jesus as the teacher who, by word and deed, reveals a new law of love to the church. Luke, in his two-volume work of Gospel and Acts, goes about the task of the theologian by showing his gentile church the marvelous continuity between the life of Jesus and the life of the church as the Spirit moved the mission of Jesus and his disciples from Galilee to Jerusalem to Rome. And John, the most evident theologian of all, depicts a masterful faith portrait of Jesus as the Word, the revealer of the Father.

This rich diversity of the New Testament books is a testimony to the power of the Spirit unleashed in the church through Jesus' resurrection. The message of the Christian church was no longer simply the same as Jesus had preached. Now the very person and work of Jesus himself had been caught up in the good news.

166

If continuity between the life of Jesus and the life of the church was compatible with a developing message, it also was compatible with a developing notion of precisely what shape the church itself was to take. The tone of the church's life was bound to change as it moved from the relatively homogeneous group of Jewish men and women who were the original witnesses of the resurrection out into vastly different cultures and places.

First of all, the very structures of the church would have to change as culture and time left their inevitable traces. The first generation of Christians obviously could afford to have a rather loose organizational structure. It was by no means totally egalitarian, even at that early date. The early chapters of Acts leave no doubt that Peter, the leader of the Apostles, and James, a relative of Jesus, were very much in charge of the Jerusalem church. They made important policy decisions, such as validating Paul's mission to the gentiles, and they kept a close watch over the orthodoxy of new groups coming into the church (cf. Acts 8:14 where Peter and John go to check on the Samaritan converts). Paul too does not hesitate to assert his teaching authority when he writes to his convert communities. But this evidence is a far cry from the concern with authority and structure implied in later New Testament writings, such as the pastoral epistles to Timothy and Titus or the second letter of Peter. Most scholars would date these epistles toward the last decade of the first century. They reflect a church that has developed considerably from the rather casual organization of the first decades of the church's life. There is a marked emphasis on tradition and correct teaching. The succession of authority in the church and the various roles the leaders are to play are more cleanly laid out. Requirements for ecclesiastical office are carefully detailed.

Such development was necessary for the church's survival. Unless it had evolved into a church with a firmer sense of its own doctrine and more definite lines of authority and communication, it might not have withstood the stresses of time and an often hostile environment.

The same is true of the inner life of the church: its piety and its way of doing things. It was all right for the first Christians to continue their normal Jewish religious customs of regular attendance at the Temple and the usual cycle of morning and evening prayers, as the early chapters of Acts inform us. But what would happen when the church took hold in Egypt or Syria or Corinth or Rome, places and peoples for whom such patterns of Jewish religious life meant very little? What would the church do when the Temple no longer existed and when the guiding force of the Jerusalem church would be swept away in the ashes of the Roman invasion of 70 A.D.? Here, again, survival demanded flexibility, adaptation, development.

The basic thrusts of this developing Christian life were surely set by Jesus' own teaching and by reflection on the meaning of his death and resurrection. The Eucharist had its roots in Jesus' last meal with his disciples and in those many fellowship meals shared with friends throughout the course of his ministry. The other sacraments, too, found their rudimentary forms in the life and ministry of Jesus: Baptism, an incorporation into Christian life, just as the baptism by John had marked the beginning of Jesus' ministry; the Anointing of the Sick, reflecting Jesus' own ministry of healing; Confirmation and Reconciliation, sacraments that marked the life of the Christian with the same life-giving Spirit that animated Jesus; Matrimony and Orders, signs of the church's concern for the critical moments of its people's lives, just as Jesus had shared in the festive joy of Cana and had blessed the commitment of his followers with a share in his own mission.

But in none of these cases had the early church received a neat kit of instructions from Jesus. The significance of these moments of grace became clear only as the church's understanding of its own power and life developed. And the ways in which the church came to use and interpret these signs of its own life would change and evolve as it marched across that inevitable threshold of time and culture.

Beyond the New Testament

The gradual development in doctrine and patterns of life that marked the first decades of the church's life did not come to a halt when the last page of the New Testament was written. The process spilled over the frontier of the New Testament period and continued throughout the centuries of the church's existence, even until today. If at any time the church had been unwilling or unable to adapt and change, it would have atrophied and died.

There is no question that the first century of its life, the period in which the New Testament writings were produced, is a special period that cannot be duplicated. The church does not continue to produce Gospels, epistles, and tracts that have the same authority as these early writings. These were the writings in proximate contact with early witnesses and traditions about Jesus. The Spirit of God who so animated the early period of the church has touched these first writings with a power and authority given to no other since. Every subsequent statement of saint or scholar must draw on these as sources of Christian truth.

But in the centuries since the New Testament period, the church has not stood still, either in what it says or in what it does. The church continued to reflect on the meaning of Jesus' death and resurrection. And it tried to articulate its maturing belief in a way that would be credible and understandable to new cultural situations. In fact, it was not until the great ecumenical Council of Nicea in 325 A.D. that the church was able to articulate clearly its belief in the divinity of Christ. Certainly a firm belief in Christ's divinity antedated the fourth century. It is a supposition of the New Testament writings and the teachings of the early Fathers of the church. But not until almost 300 years after the death of Jesus, not until the church had to confront erroneous teaching that seemed to threaten a fundamental instinct of its faith, did it use the precise tools of Greek philosophy to develop its understanding of what it meant when it confessed that Christ is divine and that God is Trinity. It would be even later, in great councils like Chalcedon in 451 A.D., that the church would turn to other fundamental questions such as the Incarnation and the relationship of Jesus' humanity and divinity and be able to articulate these doctrines in a coherent fashion. The same basic process, although not always involving such fundamental questions as these, continued in the many councils and formulations of doctrine that punctuate the long history of the church down to the present day.

What is true of the church's teaching is also true of it's way of life. The structure and piety of the medieval church in Europe vastly differed in tone from that of the Corinthian church of Paul's day. And the church of 20th-century America is hardly identical with the Byzantine church of the fifth and sixth centuries. The ways the leaders of the church exercised their authority, the ways the church prayed and celebrated its sacraments have experienced enormous changes across the spectrum of time. And even within identical periods of time, different cultures bring different expressions to church life. Change, no matter how traumatic it might be for those who swing on its hinges, has never been absent from the church of Jesus.

Back to Jesus

The emphasis in our bird's-eye view of church history has been on continuity. The evolution that began with the first moment of the church's life was not a betrayal of the teaching of Jesus but a sure sign of the presence of the Spirit. To change and adapt was a sign that the church was alive, that it was willing to bear the responsibility of deepening its understanding of who Jesus was and to proclaim this maturing faith in fresh language to all generations and cultures.

But to imply by our blessing of change that the church has marched through the centuries with unswerving fidelity to the life and teaching of its Master would be an illusion. Not all of the church's teaching over the centuries can be characterized honestly as a wise unfolding of the implications of Jesus' teaching. Many expressions of the church's prayer and piety were not really faithful translations of Christian life into new cultures and new times. And not all of the power that church authority assumed nor the styles in which it was exercised have been compatible with the teaching of Jesus, no matter what allowance is made for the context of custom and culture.

Even some of its more successful developments exacted a toll from the church. Certainly it was good that the pain and division inflicted on the church by three centuries of intermittent Roman persecution came to an end in the fourth century when the Emperor Constantine was converted and made peace with Christians. But the edict of Milan in 313 A.D. also began an unholy embrace between state and church that would hobble the freedom of the Gospel down to our own day. It was good too that the church adapted its Eucharistic worship to the culture of its people. But sometimes that adaptation meant over-assimilation of Byzantine court ritual, or gradual suffocation by piling up gestures and prayers whose original purpose often was long forgotten by the people who used them. It was necessary that the church organize itself and maintain a brisk sense of its own authority. But that often meant aping the muscular power of the state; before too long, it was hard to tell the difference between Pope and Caesar—neither of whom looked very much like Jesus of Nazareth. And it was right that the church use the power of reason and reflection in order to express its faith in terms understandable to succeeding generations. But it was not right that the church should forget the limits of human language, as it sometimes did, and delude itself into thinking that its formulations successfully bottled the mystery of the Gospel. And it makes sense that the church of Jesus should correct the errors of its members and protect its responsibility to preach the Gospel. But, too often, the zeal of some in the church became fanatical and their response to error so tainted with cruelty and ambition that the cure was less compatible with the spirit of Jesus than the ill it sought to remedy.

So not all the church's development was in the right direction. Some of it was not a step forward but a step backward. The church, like the first disciples, has not always been able to understand who Jesus is. Perhaps the most critical aspect of the church's history is found here—in its understanding of Jesus. That is its prime task in every age; that is the constant goal of its pilgrimage. Ultimately, the efficiency of the church's structures and the style of its authority are quite secondary to its ability to discover and proclaim the Risen Jesus in its midst.

Like everything else about our very human church, the record is mixed. Against the heresy of Arianism in the fourth century, the church nobly maintained its belief in the divinity of Jesus. That was absolutely necessary; otherwise our Christian heritage would have been robbed of one of the most fundamental assertions of its faith. But a strong reaction to this error and others like it tilted popular piety towards a conception of Jesus that would grow increasingly remote and divinized. The awesome power of the *Christus Pantocrator* that decorated the domed canopies of Byzantine churches and the fearsome Christ of Judgment that dominates the portals of medieval Europe's Gothic cathedrals undoubtedly find some justification in the biblical portrait of Jesus. But the dominating tone of this view of Jesus tended to eclipse the palpable humanity of the Gospel Jesus whose most evident characteristics were compassion and love, not condemning judgment.

Again and again in church history, the church's better instincts have attempted to refocus its image of Jesus. Francis of Assisi's emphasis on the humanity of Jesus in the early 13th century refreshed a church whose life was parched by dry theology and stilted piety. The tragic division of the Reformation in the 16th century jolted a complacent and often corrupt church to stir itself again to renewal. Pietistic movements in the 18th century and at the beginning of our own also were attempts of the church to find its own soul by turning again to the Gospel portrait of Jesus. We too have been victims and beneficiaries of the church's perennial struggle to be true to its heritage. The strongest impulse of the reform begun at the Second Vatican Council has been a renewed acquaintance with the biblical Jesus.

To capsulize the many centuries of the church's life, as we have done, and to attempt to isolate the causes and trends that have shaped its history can be dangerously simplistic. History, like life itself, is more complex than our analysis permits. Our observations often can result in caricature rather than insight. Where we make confident connections between cause and effect, there may be none at all. Where we eagerly tie together principle and action, the only bond may have been accident. The early church probably became a universal religion open to all not only because of Paul's eloquent arguments about the rights of the gentiles and their freedom from the obligations of the Jewish Law but because an invading Roman army annihilated both Jews and Jewish Christians in Jerusalem and thus effectively silenced that end of the debate. The Reformation and the Counter Reformation took place not only because churchmen on both sides confessed their sins and repented but because political and economic interests found division expedient. The contemporary call for reform in the past decade of Catholic life is due not only to a renewal of biblical studies and theology but to the mood of personalism and to the styles of authority that have swept over all aspects of modern life.

To admit the free play of such causes in the church's long history does not rule out the guiding presence of the Spirit. The Spirit of God works in God's ways, which are not always our own. God's ways might include the pressure of economics as well as a principle of theology. But, above all, God's way, and thus the presence of the Spirit, is detectable in the church's constant love for its Scriptures. Over and over again, when circumstances forced reform on the church—or, less frequently, when she freely chose it—the church has turned to the Word of God to renew its life. There, in the portrait of Jesus, it finds refreshment and challenge. There it finds direction for its own ministry of teaching, of healing, of reconciling.

This observation merely repeats what Luke said much more eloquently at the close of his Gospel. Two disciples hurry away from Jerusalem back home to Emmaus. They are dejected. Their hopes have been deflated by the hostility of their own people. A cruel accident of history had snuffed out the light of their lives. There was nothing left to stay around for. But, unrecognized by them, Jesus himself joins the pilgrims. He invites them to read the Scriptures, to find there the meaning of their lives and refreshment for their hope. In listening carefully to those Scriptures and in breaking bread with that mysterious pilgrim, the disciples discovered the Risen Lord in their midst.

Luke surely meant that story for his church. There would be many disciples who would be disillusioned and find no reason to stay with the rest in Jerusalem. But the remedy still held: To search the Scriptures and to pray —and to discover again the Risen Jesus. That is the purpose of the Gospels, and that is their power—for Luke's church and for our own.

Further Reading

Readers interested in doing further study on Jesus and the New Testament might find some of these titles available and helpful.

On the Gospel Portrait of Jesus

Bornkamm, Günther. *Jesus of Nazareth.* New York: Harper, 1960. Hardback, 239 pages. A beautiful and sometimes demanding study of the life and teaching of Jesus by a noted German Protestant scholar.

Dodd, C.H. *The Founder of Christianity.* New York: Macmillan, 1970. Paperback, 181 pages. One of England's most renowned New Testament scholars moves through the life of Jesus and synthesizes the Gospel perspective with balance and warmth.

Hunter, A.M. *The Work and Words of Jesus.* Philadelphia: Westminster, rev. ed., 1973. Paperback, 230 pages. Rapid survey of Gospel material, written for those with little or no background in New Testament studies by British scholar.

Reumann, John. *Jesus in the Church's Gospels. Modern Scholarship and the Earliest Sources.* Philadelphia: Fortress Press, 1973. Paperback, 539 pages. This massive work by a well-known American Lutheran scholar contains a wealth of material on the various facets of the

Gospels. A good sourcebook for those who want to move more deeply into New Testament study but still need a steady guide.

On the Origin and Nature of the Gospels

Ashton, John. *Why Were the Gospels Written?* (Theology Today Series #15). Notre Dame: Fides, 1973. Paperback, 92 pages. Answers question of title by tracing growth of the early church and illustrating how the Gospel material developed. Good representation of current Catholic thought on the question of history and Gospels.

Lohfink, Gerhard. *The Gospels: God's Word in Human Words* (Herald Biblical Booklets). Chicago: Franciscan Herald Press, 1972. Paperback, 68 pages. This work, similar to Ashton's, gives more attention to the various literary forms in the Gospels. Lohfink is a German Catholic scholar.

Mitton, C. Leslie. *Jesus: The Fact Behind the Faith*. Grand Rapids: Eerdmans, 1974. Paperback, 152 pages. Mitton cautions those who too quickly dismiss the historical accuracy of the Gospel accounts. Excellent discussion of the problem, and a persuasive presentation of a moderate and informed view on how history and interpretation blend in the Gospels.

On the World of Jesus and the Gospels

Bruce, F.F. *New Testament History*. Garden City: Doubleday, 1971. Hard and paperback editions, 462 pages. Excellent synthesis of the history of Jesus' time and of the setting of the early church by well-known British historian and New Testament scholar.

Bruce, F.F. *Jesus and Christian Origins Outside of the New Testament*. Grand Rapids: Eerdmans, 1974. Paperback, 216 pages. Examines non-biblical writings and documents to see what information they give us about Jesus and the early church. Early Roman documents, Jewish writings, and other materials are carefully evaluated.

Kee, H.C. *The Origins of Christianity, Sources and Documents*. Englewood Cliffs: Prentice-Hall, 1973. Paperback, 270 pages. Helpful collection of ancient texts and documents dealing with the New Testament and the development of the early church. Kee offers a running commentary on the pertinence of these non-biblical materials for New Testament interpretation.

Schultz, H.J. (ed.). *Jesus in His Time*. Philadelphia: Fortress Press, 1971. Paperback, 148 pages. Collection of articles originally published in German that deal with historical background of Jesus and the early church.

On the Ministry and Death of Jesus

Hunter, A.M. *The Parables Then and Now*. Philadelphia: Westminster, 1971. Paperback, 128 pages. Clearly written, popular treatment of the parables with a number of leads for contemporary interpretation of their meaning.

Schnackenburg, Rudolf. *God's Rule and Kingdom*. New York: Herder & Herder, 1963. Hardback, 365 pages. German Catholic New Testament scholar offers an informative survey of the biblical use of theme of the Kingdom in both Old and New Testaments.

Schnackenburg, Rudolf. *The Church in the New Testament*. New York: Seabury Press, 1974. Paperback, 222 pages. Author studies general characteristics of the church in the New Testament, and then he turns to the distinctive presentations of the church in each of the main New Testament authors.

Sloyan, Gerard S. *Jesus on Trial, The Development of the Passion Narratives and Their Historical and Ecumenical Implications*. Philadelphia: Fortress Press, 1973. Paperback, 156 pages. Father Sloyan works from an ecumenical perspective in examining the difficult problem of the historical circumstances surrounding Jesus' trial. Book presumes a somewhat advanced knowledge of biblical studies.

Vanhoye, Albert, S.J. *Structure and Theology of the Accounts of the Passion in the Synoptic Gospels.* Collegeville: The Liturgical Press, 1967. Paperback, 37 pages. Handy booklet offers succinct summary of how each synoptic evangelist presents the sufferings and death of Jesus.

Weiser, Alfons. *The Miracles of Jesus Then and Now.* (Herald Biblical Booklets) Chicago: Franciscan Herald Press, 1972. Paperback, 44 pages. Solid treatment of the meaning of miracles in the Gospel tradition by a German Catholic scholar.

Guillet, Jacques. *The Consciousness of Jesus.* New York: Newman Press, 1972. Paperback, 216 pages. French Catholic scholar examines various titles and images applied to Jesus in the Gospels and attempts to see how these affirmations might have been understood by Jesus and his disciples in the light of the Old Testament and first-century Judaism. A demanding book at times that has a number of valuable insights.

General Reference Works
On the Gospels and the New Testament

One of the best and most comprehensive single-volume commentaries on both Old and New Testaments is *The Jerome Biblical Commentary.* Englewood Cliffs: Prentice Hall, 1968, edited by Raymond E. Brown, S.S., Joseph A. Fitzmyer, S.J., Roland E. Murphy, O. Carm. This massive work (889 pages) includes extensive commentaries on each book of the Bible as well as major articles on individual questions such as Inspiration, Pauline Theology, Interpreting the Scriptures, and so on. For those who want to do serious reading and study of the Scriptures, this is a worthwhile investment.

Another fine Catholic commentary series on the Bible is The Liturgical Press' *Old and New Testament Reading Guides*. These paperback guides provide a detailed commentary on individual books of Old and New Testaments. Entire series is now complete.

The Franciscan Herald Press has inaugurated another popular series of commentaries and studies on biblical topics under Catholic auspices. The *Herald Biblical Booklets* study particular questions in biblical interpretation or provide background on individual books of the Bible. Several titles are now available, and more are scheduled to appear. The *Read and Pray* series offers an up-to-date commentary on individual books of the Bible plus an orientation to reflection and prayer. Studies of each of the four Gospels have appeared, and more titles are planned.

Readers looking for articles on a variety of biblical topics will appreciate *The Bible Today Reader*. Collegeville: The Liturgical Press, 1973. Paperback, 424 pages. This is a selection of articles that appeared in *The Bible Today* over the past 10 years, covering both Old and New Testaments.

Those looking for background information on specific topics within the Bible, or for information on biblical names or places, etc., will find a valuable aid in John L. McKenzie's *Dictionary of the Bible*. Milwaukee: Bruce, 1965. Paperback, 954 pages.

For a rich treatment of biblical themes and biblical theology, consult Xavier Léon-Dufour's *Dictionary of Biblical Theology*. New York: The Seabury Press, 2nd rev. ed., 1973.